Stories in Stone

View from Bishopsgate looking westward

Dedication

We wish to offer this book as a tribute to the
life and work of the publisher, the late David Herbert,
son of a former bishop of Norwich.
His skill and heartfelt enthusiasm have brought
to fruition a work in which he invested
so much of himself.

Stories in Stone

The Medieval Roof Carvings
of Norwich Cathedral

Martial Rose and
Julia Hedgecoe

Thames and Hudson

First published in paperback in the United
States of America in 1997 by Thames and
Hudson Inc., 500 Fifth Avenue, New York,
New York 10110

Published by arrangement with
The Herbert Press, London

Library of Congress Catalog in Publication
Number 96-61180

ISBN 0-500-27937-3

Editor: Curigwen Lewis
Designed by Pauline Harrison
Printed and bound in Hong Kong

front cover

The Fall (NA11)

The centre boss in the first bay of the
nave is of the temptation of Adam and
Eve in the garden of Eden. On either side
are smaller carvings – of the creation of
Adam (NA12) to the north, and of the
creation of Eve (NA10) to the south. The
tree of knowledge is covered with pointed
green leaves and an abundance of golden
apples. The trunk of the tree is set in a
round stand which in a dramatic context
might make it readily portable. Satan
is disguised: his lower half a serpent; his
upper half is that of a female with curled
hair and small breasts. The apples passed
from one to another indicate the passage
of *one* apple from Satan to Eve to Adam.
Eve is composed but Adam's eyes are
wide-open with alarm.

back cover

The vaulting of the easternmost bay of the nave (Bay NA)

The original Norman nave completed in
1144 comprised fourteen bays. The stone
vaulting, which was introduced after the
fire of 1463, was in the lierne style. This
called for a great number of short ribs
having decorative rather than structural
significance. Wherever the ribs meet keystones are required. Within each bay there
are twenty-four keystones forming a stellar pattern. Of these twenty-four keystones six, three placed on either side at
the extreme ends of the central transverse
rib, are carved on the underside with foliate or floral designs. These six bosses are
not shown in the photograph, which
shows how the other eighteen carvings are
devoted to the main story of the bay,
namely God creating the world and the
fall of man. The narrative told within the
vaulting of the fourteen bays is that of the
creation of the world to the last judgement: the first seven bays are devoted to
the Old Testament and the second set
of seven bays tells the story of the New
Testament, culminating in the last judgement at the very west end.

In the first bay the bosses show God's
work of creation: the first light, angels in
adoration, the fish, the eagle, the swan, the
hart, the creation of Adam and Eve, and
God blessing his creation. The centre
boss, a little larger than the rest, shows
Satan with a snaky tail wrapped round the
tree and a distinctly feminine head and
bosom, tempting Adam and Eve in the
Garden of Eden. The last boss in this bay
depicts the apocryphal death of Cain and
looks forward to the group of bosses in
the next bay which tells of God's sending
the flood and saving only Noah and his
family.

In succeeding bays it is the centre boss
that announces the main narrative theme
for the bay: the satellite bosses contribute
to that theme. In the main the reading of
the bosses requires the head to be turned
towards the centre: at the east end of this
bay one is looking west, and at the west
end one is looking east.

Contents

The Stone Vaults of
Norwich Cathedral
7

The Cloisters
23

The Nave Roof Bosses
51

The Bauchun Chapel and the Presbytery
87

The Transepts
107

Drama and the Roof Bosses
123

Acknowledgements
141

Bibliography
141

List of Illustrations
143

Index
143

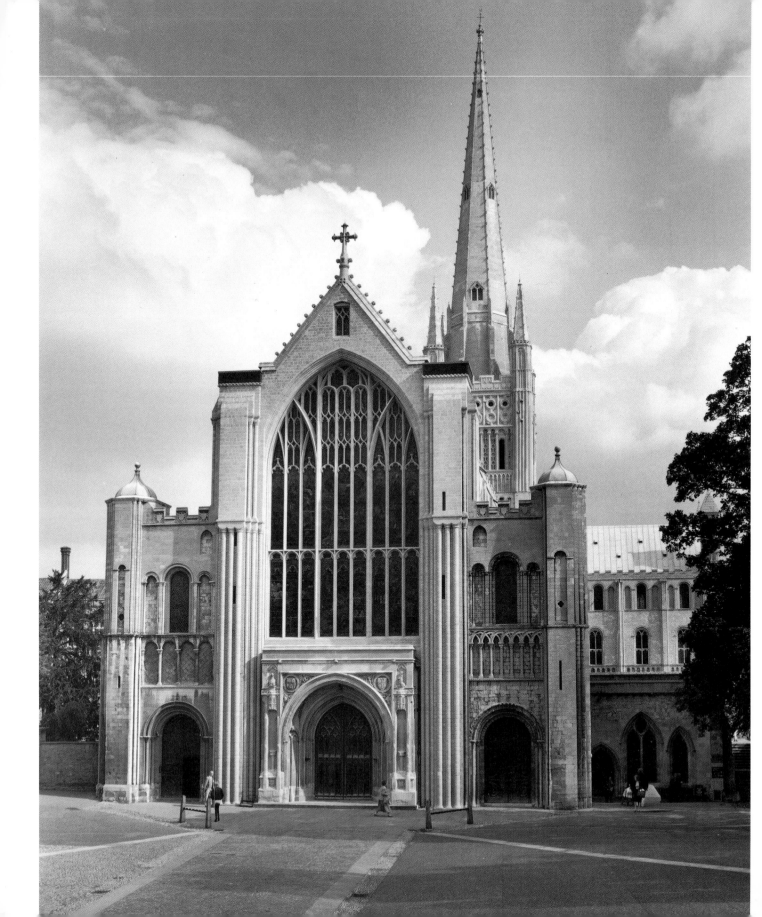

The Stone Vaults of
Norwich Cathedral

opposite
The west front

NORWICH Cathedral was founded by Bishop Herbert de Losinga in 1096. Thirty years after the Conquest the Normans had established a major fortification in Norwich and looked to develop the area as a leading trading centre. As the town grew rapidly the former see of East Anglia at Thetford was moved there. Bishop Herbert, a dedicated churchman and vigorous administrator, died in 1119 when the cathedral church, begun at the east end, had reached as far as the fourth of what had been planned as a fourteen-bay nave. The completion of the church came in 1144 under Herbert's successor, Bishop Eborard. A magnificent building, without parallel in the region, had been completed in less than fifty years. In addition, the Bishop's palace attached to the north side of the cathedral, and the Benedictine monastery with its chapter house, dormitories, refectory, cloisters and the many service areas were completed at about the same time.

The roofing of the cathedral was a gabled timber construction open to the eye from the ground. It is possible that a stone vault was erected over the eastern apse of the presbytery, the area of the cathedral treated with the greatest respect. Elsewhere English oak shed its covering over French stone. As Norfolk had no good building stone the Normans brought it from French quarries in Caen. It came at great cost by ship, across the Channel to Yarmouth, along the river Yare and its tributary, the river Wensum, to Norwich. Adjacent to the building site a canal was cut to transport the stone to within yards of where it was to be laid. Barnack stone from the quarries near Stamford, Lincolnshire, was also used. Today one can see how the Caen and Barnack stone have frequently been

LOCATING THE BOSSES

Numbers and letters in brackets indicate the position of each boss in the roof vaulting. For further clarification see the plans and notes in each chapter.

used alternately in the columns, creating a pattern of different colours: the lighter Caen against the darker Barnack. But in Norman times the pillars would have been lightly plastered and painted over and there would have been few parts of the cathedral, wood or stone, that would not have been decorated with geometric patterns or with figural work.

The wooden roofs of the cloisters and the cathedral, and also the wooden spire that rose above the majestic stone tower above the crossing, were to prove vulnerable areas: the roofs to fire, and the spire to the searching wind. But such vulnerability brought about the introduction of stone vaulting and the creation of over a thousand roof bosses which is the subject of this book. The riots of 1272, when the townsfolk set fire to the cathedral and the monastic premises, resulted in a massive rebuilding programme, part of which, between 1300 and 1450, saw the completion of the new cloisters, vaulted in stone and studded with nearly four hundred roof bosses. Lightning struck the roof of the nave in 1463 and set it ablaze, and also brought down the spire crashing onto the presbytery roof. The subsequent extensive repairs were to introduce stone vaulting into both of these areas, creating stellar patterns which required a further four hundred and sixty-four roof bosses. The Bauchun Chapel was reroofed in the 1470s with the addition of forty-seven bosses, and after the 1509 transept fire the vaulting campaign reached its final stage. The bishop at the time, Richard Nykke, was to maintain the example set by his predecessors since 1300 by installing stone vaulting richly decorated with a multiplicity of cunningly carved keystones. When this bishop died in 1536, disgraced, blind, the King's debtor in the Marshalsea prison, the Reformation was taking its toll of the old beliefs and the old forms of church embellishment. The shrines of saints were destroyed, holy statues cast from their niches, vestments and illuminated service books burnt, paintings destroyed or concealed with a wash. The day of the decorative roof boss had passed.

A stone roof boss is a keystone which holds in place the ribs of the vaulting. In the construction of the vaulting the ribs, which mostly spring from capitals of the pillars below, are held in position by a system of

previous page
Green Man (CEM5)

This remarkable, haunting image is among
the very first carvings in the east walk of
the cloisters showing a human face. It
appears towards the south end of the walk
in the midst of a group of foliate bosses.
It is as though, suddenly, from the depths
of the forest, hidden by the fronds, peers
this Green Man. His face is masked by
hawthorn leaves, like the Green Man
carved above a capital in the chapter house
of Southwell Minster. Hawthorn, or may,
as it is sometimes called, puts forth its
blossom, traditionally, on the first day of
May, a time for May games, and May
dances around the maypole. These are
folk customs predating Christianity. The
image of the Green Man is associated
with such seasonal and pagan rites.

scaffolding called centring. The keystone is lowered into position until
its angled ends lock into those of the receiving ribs. The meeting point
might be of four ribs or as many as twelve. Once the keystone is in place
the spaces between the ribs, called webs, can be filled in with stone or
sometimes brick. Although initial sculptural work on the underside of
the boss might be carried out in the mason's workshop, the completion
of the boss would have to be undertaken once the boss was *in situ*. Wooden
bosses, however, such as those above the quire in Winchester Cathedral,
are not essential parts of the vaulting structure and therefore can be completed at ground level and then literally nailed into place.

Although roof bosses are to be found in the vaulting of some Norman
churches their decorative effect is negligible. It was the advent of the more
elaborate Gothic vaulting from the end of the thirteenth century with its
profusion of carved keystones that created a striking new feature in both
ecclesiastical and secular architecture. The noble patron whose wealth
contributed to church, convent or cathedral would ensure that no less
attention and skill went to adorn his own palace or castle.

The earliest carvings are of leaves and flowers. Subsequently, figures of
Green Men, dragons and griffins appear as neighbours to the saints and
martyrs. Pre-Christian and Christian symbols inhabit the same bay cheek
by jowl. And then, in Norwich Cathedral, come the great story-telling
cycles. Norwich Cathedral is not unusual in having in its Gothic vaulting a great number of carved roof bosses. Other churches and cathedrals
can match it in number or even surpass it. The unique feature of the Norwich carvings is that the majority of them tell a story: that is, they not
only in themselves have story content, but that they often form sequences,
even great cycles, of narrative. To appreciate the extent of this, comparison
must be made with other churches where narrative roof bosses appear.
Some late-thirteenth-century roof bosses in the Lady Chapel and the
presbytery of Exeter Cathedral show a hunter, a dog, the Coronation
of the Virgin, the Crucifixion, wrestlers, a dragon, and a mermaid: all
attractive, decorative, but not sequential. In the fourteenth century the
nave was vaulted and along the main ridge are a number of magnificently

carved bosses, none more so than, at the west end, the one representing the murder of Thomas Becket. This is packed with dramatic content but again stands alone. In the south walk of the cloisters of Worcester Cathedral there are two series of bosses. At the west end is a tree of Jesse and the succeeding bosses, moving east, are of the kings stemming from Jesse's line. The centre boss in this walk is of the Coronation of the Virgin. The other series, moving west, which also culminates at the centre of the walk, shows kings and prophets carrying scrolls foretelling the coming of Christ. The closest analogy to the Norwich narrative sequences is to be found in the fourteenth-century vaulting in Tewkesbury Abbey. In the nave there are three sequences of five bosses each on the Life of Christ: the Nativity, the Passion, the Resurrection.

In Norwich Cathedral the earliest sequence of narrative bosses begins in the east walk of the cloisters: a set of five on the Passion of Christ. The monks, as they made their way along this walk and into the cathedral would pass under this representation of Christ's Passion which might have served to put them into the right frame of mind for the divine service they were about to attend. The next sequence is that of the hundred carvings on the theme of the Apocalypse to be seen in the south and west walks of the cloisters. The last book of the Bible, the Revelation of St John the Divine, was commonly called the Apocalypse because it foretold in graphic, cryptic, and sometimes alarming language the afflictions that would be visited on erring mankind as the world drew towards its close. When the wooden nave roof was destroyed by fire in 1463 and Bishop Lyhart gave instructions for a stone-vaulted replacement he must also have determined the theme of the carvings. This was to show the story of the world as understood by the medieval Christian. The carvings along the vaulting of the fourteen bays depict the story of the creation of the world in the easternmost bay and continue through Old and New Testament stories, culminating with the last judgement at the nave's western extremity.

The other areas of the cathedral that were subsequently to receive stone vaulting were the Bauchun Chapel off the south ambulatory of the

overleaf
The Carrying of the Cross (CED5)

The scene is set within a wreath. Leaves reach into the middle of the boss to lap over the figure of Christ and to cover part of the torturer who holds the three spikes with which he will nail Christ to the cross. In his right hand he clutches the shaft of a substantial claw-hammer. Christ carries the cross, parts of which have broken off, over his right shoulder. He is naked apart from a drooping loin-cloth. He looks back over his right shoulder towards the torturer who holds the three heavy-headed spikes in his left hand within the right-angle made by the upright and the horizontal arms of the cross. The torturer's head is craned backwards, echoing the angle.

previous page
**A thief caught stealing
the washing** (CED4)

This carving appears in the fourth bay of
the east walk. It is placed at the apex of
the arch which looks out on to the garth. In
each of the bays of this walk there are
eight roof bosses. The centre boss in this
bay is that of Christ carrying his cross to
Calvary. Lions are carved in four of the
other bosses. Another depicts a squint-
eyed Green Man. St Luke and his symbol,
a calf, is carved above the wall arch, opposite the one illustrated here. The range of
subjects is typical of the north end of this
east walk: biblical, animal, foliate, pagan,
and the stuff of folk stories.

This scene probably represents a woman
who has caught a thief attempting to steal
her washing. This was one of the avowed
peccadilloes of Autolycus in *The Winter's
Tale* and the sort of mischief that Puck in
A Midsummer-Night's Dream might have
played on 'the maidens of the villagery'.
Here however the thief has been caught
red-handed by the housewife. On her head
she wears a white wimple. Her long light-
brown gown reaches to her feet. A pointed
shoe is firmly placed upon one of the garments the thief is trying to take. The
woman's right arm is raised above her
shoulder as though she is preparing a
heavy downward blow with a distaff or
rolling-pin on to the thief's head. Her
wrist, hand, and whatever weapon her
hand was holding have broken off. She extends her left arm – her sleeve seems to be
rolled up – so that she clutches hold of
the thief's hair. The thief who is dressed
in nothing but a pair of red and white
striped drawers, has his right foot thrust
against the woman's left breast and his left
foot on the square washing-board. With

presbytery, the presbytery roof itself, and lastly the north and south
transepts.

In the *Canterbury Tales* Chaucer's Man of Law tells a tale about the
daughter of the Emperor of Rome who is calumniated and suffers many
hardships which she survives through the constancy of her faith. A similar story is told in the roof bosses of the Bauchun Chapel, *c.*1475. The
Chapel is dedicated to Our Lady of Pity and the carvings show how the
Virgin Mary brings comfort to the Empress in her distress. The close
association of these carvings with the fifteenth-century murals behind the
choir in Eton College Chapel, which recount an analagous theme, makes
the pursuit of the narrative's origin particularly intriguing.

It would seem as though the story-telling character of the roof bosses
in Norwich Cathedral had come to an end in about 1480 when a splendid stone vault was erected in the presbytery during the episcopate of
Bishop Goldwell (1472-99). It was pitched more than ten feet higher than
the nave vaulting. In the 1360s the clerestory windows had been greatly
enlarged allowing much more light to flood into the whole presbytery
area. The new vaulting, stretching over four bays, and the apsidal east
end also received the benefit of the additional light from the enlarged
clerestory windows. The bosses in their patterned clusters appear like
stars, but the story-telling treatment has been abandoned. Of the one
hundred and twenty-eight bosses, ninety-four are of gold wells, a rebus
on the bishop's name, and others are floral or foliate. Three of the five
larger bosses along the main ridge are of the bishop's coat of arms. The
choice of subjects for the presbytery bosses shows a self-indulgence on
the part of Bishop Goldwell in his concern to be remembered in per-
petuity, but it scarcely detracts from the majestic spectacle that the vaulting creates.

The final phase of stone vaulting took place after the 1509 fire in the
transepts. It was undertaken during the episcopate of Bishop Nykke. A
stellar pattern of vaulting was constructed similar to those in the nave
and presbytery. The treatment of subject reverted to the narrative mode
but with a significant difference. Instead of a long story being told in

14

broad outline by the carvings, the method adopted in the transepts is to tell a very limited story by charting the progressive movements of the characters within it. In this way very close attention is given, for instance, to the Nativity or to the Massacre of the Innocents or to the death of John the Baptist. The subjects treated are the early lives of Jesus and John the Baptist, in the north transept, and the early ministry of Jesus and of John the Baptist, leading to the latter's death, in the south transept.

One of the most striking features of the vault bosses is their colour. The different colour ranges used in the past is of some help in interpreting the subject-matter, especially when the bosses are examined through binoculars. However, we can have little assurance that the colours seen today match those originally employed in the Middle Ages. Some records of paints used in the thirteenth and fourteenth centuries on the sculptural work within the cathedral and priory are extant. For example, payments are made for a blue paint (azur), for vermilion, green (verdigris), silver, gold, yellow/orange (saffron), and lead white. At the Reformation, and at intervals since, the vaulting was covered with a wash – white, brown, or stone-coloured, according to the requirement and taste of the period. Such washes helped to preserve much of the original paint and it is probable that when Dean Goulburn removed a brown wash from the nave vaulting in the 1870s and recorded the colours of the bosses thus exposed, he was recording the original colouring. Subsequent repainting campaigns on nave and transepts, such as those of the 1930s, may have followed the original colour scheme, but to what degree the medieval spirit has been maintained in style and treatment is impossible to say without detailed analysis. A prodigious amount of gold leaf was used in the 1960s in the repainting of the vault bosses of the Bauchun Chapel, which has obscured rather than enhanced the story material therein. In 1992 the Courtauld Institute, London, reported on the repainting of the cloisters, where no original paint has been identified, and indicated the dangers of overpainting. The Institute advocated that regular cleaning rather than repainting might be the preferred method of maintaining a medieval ambience.

his left hand he still holds the left sleeve of one of the garments and with his right hand he holds aloft another. The wood grain on the washing-board has been represented in realistic detail.

The woman smiles grimly at her ascendancy; the thief with open mouth and startled eyes receives his come-uppance. A cautionary tale!

overleaf

Man fighting a dragon (CEF3)

This carving is to be found in the east walk of the cloisters in the sixth bay beyond the Prior's Door. The carving was undertaken in the very first years of the fourteenth century and represents symbolically the struggle between good and evil. The theme of man fighting lions, bears, griffins, and dragons is frequently depicted in medieval art and occurs within the cloister carvings on a number of occasions.

The young protagonist is dressed in a full red cloak which sweeps over his right shoulder. He has dark wavy hair and black eyes. With his left hand he clutches at the ridged back of the dragon and with his right hand he thrusts into the dragon's mouth what appears to be a substantial section of his sword. The sword has a golden hilt, a short hand-guard, and a grooved blade. The dragon's head is smaller than the man's. It has red, fiery eyes, large extended wings, and it places one clawed foot on the man's left thigh and the other on his forehead.

previous page
The tumbler (CEF6)

This carving is to be found in the east walk of the cloisters in the sixth bay from the Prior's Door. This was the first walk of the cloisters to be repaired after the riots of 1272. The carving probably dates from the very first years of the fourteenth century and is one of the earliest figure carvings in the cloister. It shows what might be a young acrobat in a contorted position with his legs bent beneath him and his arms extended above his head. He has long flowing hair which, with his position and the treatment of the drapes in his garment, gives the impression of flying movement, almost like that of a trapeze artist. The painting of this boss in 1989 revealed the powdered effect of red paint, three dots in a triangular pattern, on the surface of the green garment. It was further revealed that this tumbler is wearing gloves and these too have a red pin-point pattern on them.

overleaf
St John and the angel (CSC2)

'After these things I saw, and behold, a door opened in heaven, and the first voice which I heard, a voice as of a trumpet speaking with me, one saying, Come up hither, and I will show thee the things which must come to pass hereafter.'

Rev. 4. 1.

St John on the left and the angel on the right are borne aloft on white clouds

Cathedral and priory records also provide names of many of the masons, the payments made to them, and the additional grants they enjoyed such as gloves, gowns, and bedding. Many of the masons had experience of working elsewhere on important projects: at St Paul's Cathedral, London, on St Stephen's Chapel, Westminster, on the octagon tower of Ely Cathedral, at Eton College, at King's College Chapel, Cambridge. Much of the workmanship on the Norwich roof bosses is of the highest quality but some of it is crude, perhaps the work of an apprentice. Apart from the carving in the cloisters and the Bauchun Chapel, the height of the carving from the ground makes the story detail indecipherable by the human eye. Nevertheless the most lofty work is as carefully carved and skilfully finished as any at a lower level. This reflects not just a feeling of self-respect on the part of the sculptor but a belief that his work was an essential part of the whole building of the church which was for the worship and praise of God. When, at the Reformation, that mode of worship was put in question and so much of the artistic embellishments destroyed as being conducive to superstition and idolatry, it was the inaccessibility of the roof bosses which helped to preserve them from the hand of the vandal. For that posterity has much to be thankful for.

below and on either side of them. They stand in front of a building with an open doorway with a cusped arch, with further arches to left and right. St John with his right hand holds the side of a ladder. With his left hand he gestures upwards. He is in the process of climbing the ladder to heaven; his left foot is on the second rung; his right foot rests on the clouds. The angel points upwards with two fingers of his right hand towards heaven.

opposite
Norwich Cathedral and Priory: plan adapted from the original by Arthur Whittingham, reproduced courtesy of Jarrold Publishing.

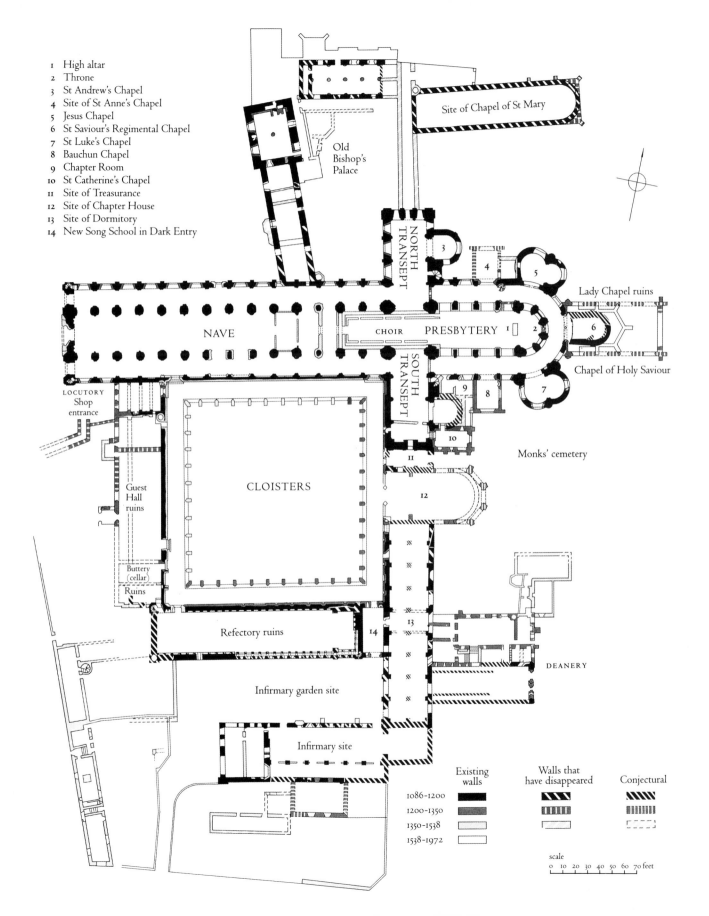

1 High altar
2 Throne
3 St Andrew's Chapel
4 Site of St Anne's Chapel
5 Jesus Chapel
6 St Saviour's Regimental Chapel
7 St Luke's Chapel
8 Bauchun Chapel
9 Chapter Room
10 St Catherine's Chapel
11 Site of Treasurance
12 Site of Chapter House
13 Site of Dormitory
14 New Song School in Dark Entry

Site of Chapel of St Mary

Old
Bishop's
Palace

NORTH TRANSEPT

NAVE

CHOIR   PRESBYTERY   1   2

SOUTH TRANSEPT

Lady Chapel ruins

6

Chapel of Holy Saviour

3

4

5

9   8

7

10

11

Monks' cemetery

LOCUTORY
Shop
entrance

Guest
Hall
ruins

Buttery
(cellar)
Ruins

CLOISTERS

12

13

14

Refectory ruins

DEANERY

Infirmary garden site

Infirmary site

	Existing walls	Walls that have disappeared	Conjectural
1086-1200			
1200-1350			
1350-1538			
1538-1972			

scale
0 10 20 30 40 50 60 70 feet

previous page
The opening of the fourth seal (CSF1)

'And when he had opened the fourth seal, I heard the voice of the fourth living creature saying, Come. And I saw, and behold a pale horse: and he that sat upon him, his name was Death; and Hades followed with him. And there was given unto them authority over the fourth part of the earth, to kill with sword, and with famine, and with death, and by the wild beasts of the earth.'

Rev. 6. 7, 8.

At the top of the boss is the head of the fourth living creature, the calf, with the end of a scroll in its mouth, and the other end held by its right forefoot. The calf is winged and its left wing forms the background, together with white clouds, for the head of the crowned rider who is mounted on the 'pale horse'. The rider's right arm is broken off. A sword would have been held in the right hand. The horse appears to be riding out of the jaws of hell, which are wide open showing an array of grinding and piercing teeth. The mouth of hell is depicted as part of the head of the fierce, wide-eyed Leviathan, as in the Harrowing of Hell (CEA5) or the Mouth of Hell (NN4).

Cloister west walk

The Cloisters

WHEN a monastic establishment was attached to a cathedral church, the cloisters were usually built on the south side of the cathedral and access from the monks' dormitories was often along a covered way lying to the east of the cloister leading to the south transept. This was a convenience for the monks especially at night when their first service, mattins, started as early as 2 a.m. During the day the monks found their way into the cathedral by the cloisters, through the east or west walks. The cloisters were for recreation, study, prayer, and, in the summer months, for reading. The area in the centre, the garth, was cultivated as a garden. In Norwich there are the remains of many book-cupboards set into the cloister walls, and on the stone benches lining the walls are the indentations which indicate that the monks played the game of nine men's morris, a medieval form of naughts and crosses. The southern sun fell on the north walk, an area reserved for the senior brethren.

The twelfth-century cloisters were generously proportioned – each walk was 180 ft (55m) long. A chapter house, the regular meeting place of the prior and the monks, adjoined the east walk. Over the cloisters the Normans built a wooden lean-to roof supported on the garth side by a series of twin pillars with carved capitals. Some of these capitals were found in the early 1900s embedded in the wall of the south walk, encased in later masonry. The dormitories lay to the east of the cloisters, the refectory to the south, and the reception area for visitors to the west. The events of 1272 led to the radical reconstruction of the whole area.

From the foundation of the cathedral and priory the relations between

overleaf

The angel sounds the sixth trumpet (CS15)

'And the sixth angel sounded, and I heard a voice from the horns of the golden altar which is before God, one saying to the sixth angel, which had the trumpet, Loose the four angels which are bound at the great river Euphrates. And the four angels were loosed, which had been prepared for the hour and day and month and year, that they should kill the third part of men.'

Rev. 9. 13-15

Christ with a cruciform nimbus is seated within a mandorla set against white clouds. He holds up both arms but his hands are missing. His feet rest on an orb. A vested altar stands to the right of the mandorla. Near the altar to the right are two angels the lower of which is unbinding the four angels in the river Euphrates. These four angels are standing in the river while a rope under their chins is being removed. The sixth trumpet, probably blown by the topmost angel, has broken off.

previous page
The sealing of the tomb (CNA5)

In the north walk of the cloisters is a group of bosses which may be closely associated with the *N-Town Play*. The sealing of the tomb is an action in this cycle of plays which does not appear elsewhere in the English cycles. Caiaphas, the high priest, asks Pilate to send soldiers to seal the tomb to prevent Christ's rising from it, or his disciples stealing his body away and falsely proclaiming Christ's resurrection. A stage direction indicates that Pilate, Annas and Caiaphas with all the soldiers go to the tomb; and there the tomb is sealed at the four corners. Annas also advises that the tomb should be locked. This scene is shown in the carving. Pilate is on the left of the tomb and behind him are two of his courtiers and four of his knights. In the play he designates four knights, and names them, to guard the tomb. On the right of the tomb are Annas and Caiaphas, and behind them four priests. Annas carries in his left hand a jar of wax. Behind him Caiaphas, with his gloves held in his left hand, has his right hand palm upwards on the tomb as though sealing the wax with his signet ring. In the play specific reference is made to Pilate's seal being affixed to the tomb. Pilate carries his staff in his left hand, the top of which has been broken off. At the level of his head the golden clasp of the lock of the tomb waits perhaps to be snapped to, across the mid-part of the tomb. On the lid of the tomb is a foliate cross on a stepped base.

the churchmen and the townsfolk were not good. The churchmen and the large lay community that worked within the precincts of the priory were subject to an ecclesiastical court and in the event of any misdemeanour were exempt from civil court proceedings. Furthermore great swathes of Norwich were owned by bishop or priory. Rents were paid for pasturage, tolls were taken on the waterways and for the grinding of corn. The bishop and prior were anxious that no neighbouring town mill should be established to threaten the revenues taken by their own mills. On feast days and at fairs when the townsfolk wished to erect booths in open spaces, such as Tombland, the prior invariably made swingeing charges for the privilege, fuelling the resentment of the townsfolk. When, on Trinity Sunday 1272, a citizen was killed in Tombland, probably accidentally, by one of the prior's men while tilting at a quintain (a military exercise), a crisis was pending. The prior's man was acquitted by the ecclesiastical court. The following day, one of the prior's men was killed. Rioting broke out and continued for a month. The prior invited men from Yarmouth to reinforce his own fighting establishment. Nothing could have incensed the Norwich citizens more. The prior's men mounted the top of the bell tower which at that time was adjacent to what is now the Erpingham Gate, and fired with their crossbows on the citizens and then carried out pillaging and fire-raising attacks on the town. The final response of the citizens was to climb to the spire of St George's Tombland and with combustible arrows attack the bell tower and other vulnerable wooden roofs within the cathedral and priory precincts. All was ablaze: the citizens broke through the prior's defences bent on a course of vengeful destruction.

The rebuilding that was required after the riots began with the cathedral church, which was consecrated when King Edward I and Queen Eleanor visited Norwich in 1278. The new chapter house was completed in 1293 with the three arches of its west front forming an integral part of the cloister's east walk. It is probable that the wooden roofs of the cloisters had been damaged in the 1272 riots but no scorch marks were discovered on the Norman capitals when they were brought to light earlier this century. The rebuilding of the cloisters took from 1297 to 1430 and the last pavement was laid *c.*1450. Throughout this long period of construction it must be assumed that the workmen, beginning with the east walk and moving clockwise round the cloisters, left *in situ* the Norman pillars and capitals of each walk until their building campaign was ready for that particular walk. The capitals bearing both foliate and figured work must have exerted some influence on the subsequent Gothic carving.

The cloisters retain the same spacious dimensions allotted by the Normans but the vaulting is of stone, and traceried windows look out onto the garth. The roof is mainly of Caen stone, the stepped buttresses of Barnack or Clipsham, and the slender columns, supporting the tracery, of Purbeck. Each walk except the east has eleven bays, and there are four corner bays. The larger bays adjoining the chapter house were *in situ* before work on the east walk got under way which was the reason there were twelve bays in this walk, the ones to the north being squeezed smaller than those fronting the chapter house. With only a few exceptions, in the vaulting of each bay there are eight bosses.

During the initial stages of work on the cloisters John Salmon was bishop (1299-1325) and Henry Lakenham prior (1289-1310). In an undertaking of such magnitude the design of the vaulting, the detail of the tracery, and the treatment of the roof bosses would not have been left to the whim of the master mason. As the cloisters were an integral part of the priory it might be thought that the prior would have been responsible for instructing the masons. This might have been so but in pre-Reformation times the bishop had considerably more authority regarding the management of both cathedral and priory. And indeed John Salmon left in his will a sum of money to be devoted to the continuing work on the cloisters, and other bishops, Wakering, for instance, did the same. Throughout the period of the building of the cloisters the style of the vaulting was virtually unchanged, but the patterns of the window tracery afford the architectural student a lesson on the development from the geometric phase of the Decorated style in the east walk to the curvi-

overleaf
The Serpent tempting Adam and Eve (CWAI)

When the monks went from the cloisters into the refectory for their meals they had to pass through the south-west doorway. The keystone above the arch is carved with this scene of the temptation of Adam and Eve. The area is usually so dark that the detail on this boss has remained largely indiscernible.

The boss was carved in *c.*1415, perhaps at the time that the battle of Agincourt was being fought. The leaves spread above the trees in a broad v-shape. The colouring, applied in the 1930s, shows golden leaves, and behind each leaf is a green apple. The Serpent's thin golden tail is entwined round the black trunk of the tree, and the Serpent's face is turned towards the left where Eve stands holding an apple in her right hand. Her left arm and hand have been broken off. Her hand most probably was held out towards Adam offering him another apple. On the right Adam stands clutching an apple in his right hand and holding his left hand to his breast as though beating it. Eve's stance is one of repose; Adam's indicates agitation.

The medieval mind accepted that man fell from God's grace through disobedience. The Serpent approached first the weaker vessel, Eve, and she, in turn, being beguiled, tempted Adam. One of the sins which they were committing was that of gluttony.

Perhaps it was intended that the monks should be reminded of this each time they passed through this doorway on their way to their next meal.

previous page
The Christian of Constantinople (CWJ7)

The main theme of the carving in the west walk of the cloisters is the completion of the story of the Apocalypse, begun in the south walk. Three additional stories are told in the bosses over the wall arches: St Basil's appeal to the Virgin Mary in his dealing with Julian the Apostate (four carvings); the Christian of Constantinople (three carvings); and scenes from the life of St Christopher (two carvings).

The Christian of Constantinople borrows money from a Jew and gives as his pledge a statue of the Virgin Mary. When time for repayment comes the Christian is at sea. He lowers a casket carrying the money owing into the water. The Jew, by the shore, picks up the casket but refuses to accept that the debt has been repaid. The image of the Virgin declares that payment in full has been made, and so the Jew is convicted in public.

This carving shows the second scene in this drama. There are two distinct actions: one at sea on the left; and one on land on the right. On the left is a masted ship with four men on board. The Christian of Constantinople, because it is time to pay his debt to the Jew, leans over the ship to place in the water the casket. On the right, against a background of foliage to indicate land, the Jew bends down to pick up the casket. A companion stands behind him.

linear mode in the south and west walks to the Perpendicular style seen in the north walk.

Once the chapter house had been finished and work on the east walk of the cloisters was in hand, the first part of the vaulting to be completed was that from the three bays adjoining the chapter house to the south end of the walk. There is no evidence that the subject of the roof bosses was settled at the outset of the building programme but most of this early work has foliate designs. Much of the carving is exquisite with the detail of leaf and berry accurately observed. A rich variety of leaf examples has been chosen — oak, hawthorn, vine, acanthus, bryony, maple, buttercup. The range is not, perhaps, as great as the leaves carved on the capitals in the chapter house at Southwell or at York, a few years earlier, but the tradition of naturalistic representation has been maintained with comparable skill and effectiveness. A characteristic shared with the work at York and Southwell is that the carving does not distinguish between small and large leaves, the hawthorn and the vine leaf for instance. The emphasis on foliage motifs in this first phase of the cloister bosses is to be influential as the figure carving develops.

The last few bays, as one moves southwards along the east walk, contain a few figured carvings. They are enthralling: a dragon with long pointed ears, in the midst of oak leaves, is eating acorns; from behind a frond of hawthorn leaves a Green Man peers out of his hiding place; a hybrid creature with two heads, one neck, no body and clawed feet, is set in a wreath of leaves; a cowled monk with no body but with fat haunches and cloven hooves glares down from above the tracery of the last arch in the walk. Similar images decorate the margins of illuminated manuscripts such as the *Luttrell* or *Ormesby Psalters* and the hybrid figure, part human, part animal, part foliate, appears repeatedly. These psalters are of East Anglian provenance of the first half of the fourteenth century, almost contemporary with the cloister carvings. The context of these strange images is the book of psalms, the most used service book in the Christian calendar. The illuminated capitals in the psalters mostly represent biblical events but in the margins, contrasting with Old and New Testament illustrations, is this other body of decoration of foliage, flowers, hybrids, and grotesques.

When the vaulting had been completed between the chapter house arches and the south end of the east walk, the masons, working north-wards, created some of their finest carvings. The first sequence of storied bosses in the east walk of the cloisters in the early years of the fourteenth century was an event of some significance. The theme was the Passion of Christ. It was the first of its kind, and it set an example in Norwich Ca-thedral for the development of narrative carving on a far greater scale. This sequence leads to the Prior's Door. Over the door is carved the figure of Christ enthroned, showing his five wounds. An angel with the instru-ments of his Passion stands on either side. Further to the left are St Peter and John the Baptist, and to the right are St Edmund of East Anglia, and Moses with the tablets of the ten commandments. The monks on their way to their services passed beneath the roof boss images of Christ's Passion and through the door, above which they saw Christ in judgement, flanked by the signs of the old Law and the new Law, the founder of the early church, St Peter, and one of the more recent and the most popular of local saints, St Edmund.

The series of carvings on Christ's Passion is featured in the centre bosses of the first five bays to the south of the Prior's Door. It comprises the Flagellation (CEE5), the Carrying of the Cross (CED5 p.12), the Crucifixion (CEC5), the Resurrection (CEB5), and the Harrowing of Hell (CEA5). The foliate carving predominant in the earlier bosses of this walk is an ever present feature in this Passion sequence, but here the foliage takes on a subordinate but symbolic role. In the Flagellation, for instance, the vine leaves not only circle the main carving in which Christ is bound to the trunk of a vine, but bunches of grapes appear between the scourgers and Christ, and vine leaves overlap the scourgers' tunics. This gives a fresh connotation to 'I am the true vine' (John 15. 1). In the carving of the Crucifixion foliage springs from all the extremities of the cross as though the body of Christ gives life to the dead wood. Analogies with contem-porary illuminated manuscripts are not confined to foliage, hybrids, and

overleaf
Doubting Thomas (CNB2)

'... reach hither thy hand, and put it into my side: and be not faithless, but believ-ing.'

John 20. 27.

This is one of a series of bosses in the north walk which continues the narrative of Christ's Resurrection, seen in the north end of the east walk. Two neighbouring bosses have shown Mary Magdalene en-countering Christ; in the first she mistakes him for a gardener (CNA8), and in the second she kneels at Christ's feet when she recognizes him as her risen Lord (CNB1). In it Christ draws away from Mary Magdalene as she is attempting to wipe his wounded feet with her long hair. But in this carving Christ forcefully pulls Thomas's reluctant right hand towards his wounded side. The two figures, the kneel-ing, apprehensive disciple and the curving stance of his triumphant, resurrected mas-ter, are gracefully complementary. The sculpting of the drapery underlines this relationship. The folds in Thomas's gown keep him downward on his knees; those in Christ's buoy him upwards. The back-ground is of leaves and bunches of grapes: an echo of the carvings set against wreaths which were characteristic of some of the earlier east-walk bosses.

31

previous page

The martyrdom of St Denis (CNJ7)

St Denis or St Dionysius is the patron saint of Paris. It is reported that he was sent as one of seven bishops to convert Gaul (*c.*AD 90). He was condemned to death by the Roman emperor, Domitian. In the seventh century his remains were translated to King Dagobert's foundation at St Denis, near Paris. The refashioning of this church in the twelfth century under the direction of Abbot Suger was to bring a radical reassessment of medieval ecclesiastical architecture.

On the left of this boss the mitred bishop, St Denis, kneels with his hands clasped together in prayer. Above him stands his executioner with his left hand on the bishop's mitre and his right hand raised and about to strike off his victim's head. The axe or sword once held in this hand is missing. Enthroned above the executioner is the Emperor Domitian. He is crowned, bearded, and with long hair. In his right hand he holds a sceptre. Immediately beneath the emperor is another portrayal of St Denis. This time the figure is headless. His neck-stump is bleeding. He carries his mitred head with both hands in front of him, and he is going to church. Within an extremely small space the carver has contrived to show us a building with transepts, a south aisle, a tower with a spire, and the roofing of the chancel. The roof ridges are marked with tiny crockets. At the west door of the church stands a Benedictine monk to welcome the bishop and his severed head.

grotesques. In this Passion sequence, for instance, the Carrying of the Cross can be compared with a similar image in the *Luttrell Psalter* where the torturer carrying the three spikes aloft pulls Christ after him.

The scene of the Crucifixion with Mary standing to the left of the cross and St John, holding a book, to the right is not only akin in style to such scenes in contemporary manuscripts but probably mirrors the figures on the rood screens erected across the west end of most chancels in cathedrals and parish churches throughout the country in the fourteenth and fifteenth centuries.

It is apparent that in this carving of the Crucifixion the lower limbs of Christ have been crudely replaced. The desecration of such images was a consequence of the Reformation, and in the 1640s another great wave of iconoclasm took place, spurred on by a puritanic zeal to be systematic and thorough. The heads of the images were the main targets. In the cloisters the roof bosses were the ready victims of pike and spear, especially noticeable near the doorways. Some repairs have been effected over the years by fixing a metal or wooden dowel into the neck of the decapitated figure and attaching to it a replacement plaster head. Such heads have now either fallen off or have deteriorated more than the original carving. Selection has governed some of the phases of iconoclasm because, although in this walk the Passion sequence shows evidence of deliberate damage, many other bosses of animals, of foliage, or of a pagan nature, bear little witness of the vandal's hand.

The Harrowing of Hell is the subject of the roof boss immediately south of the Prior's Door. It tells the apocryphal story of Christ's descent into hell following his death on the cross. Christ overcomes Satan and leads to heaven the souls of Adam and Eve and the prophets who have been waiting in limbo for this moment of redemption. In the carving Christ stands over a vanquished Satan in the form of a fat toad into whose rump he presses the butt of his cross-staff. He holds Adam by the right wrist and leads him out of the jaws of hell. Eve and the prophets follow. The mouth of hell is that of the dreaded sea-monster, Leviathan, with a fine set of grinding teeth and fierce canines. A broken chain hanging down from the mouth symbolizes Christ's triumph over the powers of darkness. It is anomalous that this carving should follow rather than precede the Resurrection. Another apparent anomaly is the direction of the Passion sequence. On the way to the Prior's Door the monks could not read the Passion sequence without turning their back to the door and looking southwards.

The Passion carvings in the five northernmost bays are surrounded by a great variety of other fascinating figured work: Green Men, lions, a fox with a goose, men fighting dragons, perhaps the head of a donor or one of the masons, street musicians, a woman having caught a thief stealing her washing (CED4 p.13). There are, however, a few other carvings of Christian significance: over four of the wall arches are to be seen in turn the four evangelists with their symbols and the scrolls of their gospels; and there is one badly damaged boss of the martyrdom of St Edmund, shot to death by the arrows of the Danes.

The team of masons working on the cloisters at times numbered fifteen. When resources were short the number was less and at times the work came to a halt altogether. During the winter months very little was done, mainly because the mortar would not dry during prolonged cold, damp spells. Often more than one walk was in construction at the same time. Parts of the east and south walks were built during the second and third decades of the fourteenth century; and parts of the west and north walks were completed together in the last phase, c.1425-30. The summer plague of 1349 claimed very many Norwich victims, including monks and the masons, and the whole building programme, then at the south west corner, came to an abrupt halt, and remained frozen for many years.

The subjects chosen for the bosses in the south and west walks continued to include a significant amount of foliage, and there were also in the south walk a number of hybrids. Struggles against beasts are again evident: a knight being overcome by a griffin; Samson tearing open the mouth of a lion, each glaring fiercely at the other. And three stories from the gospels are to be seen over the window arches in the south walk: John the Baptist about to have his head cut off; the Annunciation; Mary

overleaf
The swan (NA15)

In the first bay of the nave there are among God's Creation a lion, a unicorn, a white hart, a variety of fish, a magnificent eagle, and a swan. Such an assembly of creatures would often feature in an illuminated psalter on one of the early folios depicting the Creation. The swan in this Norwich boss wears a coronet around its neck and is therefore of special interest. The swan is swimming in blue water. It is white decorated with large golden spots and it has a red bill. Henry of Lancaster married Mary de Bohun in 1380 and used the de Bohun device of the white swan with a golden coronet around its neck as a badge. Later his son, the Prince of Wales, was to use it as a livery badge. It was an emblem closely associated with the House of Lancaster.

The construction of the nave vault began in the early years of Edward IV's reign in the 1460s. Edward was the eldest son of the Duke of York. It is therefore curious to see within the same bay not only the sun of York as the very first boss, no doubt in this position signifying also God's first created light, and also, so very near it, the swan with the gorged coronet, such a well-known symbol of the House of Lancaster.

35

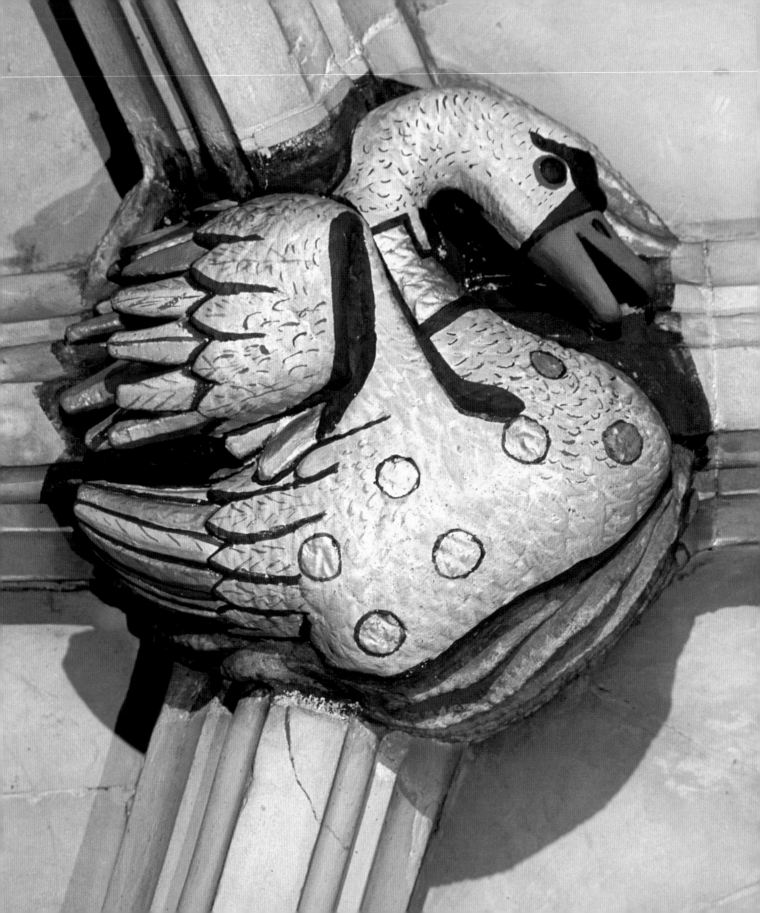

previous page
The eagle (NA16)

This magnificent eagle is seen in the vaulting of the first bay in the nave. It is among God's first created creatures. Its wings are half-spread, its head is directed forward, and its open beak, fierce eye and the latent movement of its whole form indicate that it has its prey in sight. The colours black, red, and gold almost certainly follow those of the original painting, detailed by Dean Goulburn when the brown wash covering the roof bosses was removed in the 1870s. The ripple effect on either side above the eagle represents clouds. The blue and white colours for the sky spill over the edges of the ribs. This is not carelessness on the part of the painter but a device to widen the background of the carving. It occurs a few times in this first bay, but is extensively used some years later in the painting of the presbytery bosses.

visiting her cousin, Elizabeth. However, the south and west walks are noted for containing the first sustained cycle of carvings on the Apocalypse. They number over one hundred: thirty-eight are located in the south walk and sixty-four in the west walk. If an instruction to carve this cycle was given to the masons by bishop or prior, as is most likely, then the original plan was probably to complete the series of a hundred carvings, but spreading the work along the main ridge of the vaulting, in each of the three remaining walks, allowing approximately thirty carvings for each walk. If so, such a scheme was maintained in the south walk but abandoned after the first four bays in the west walk. From this point the number of Apocalypse carvings along the central ridge increases, in addition to the theme being taken up on either side of the central ridge. There is a manifest effort to complete the series at the north end of the west walk.

The courage and imagination of bishop and prior in choosing to undertake such a cycle of carving cannot be exaggerated. As far as we know there was no precedent in church iconography for such a scheme at that time. There were of course a number of magnificent illuminated manuscripts of the Apocalypse, to some of which bishop and prior would certainly have had access. Such work was so popular that over ninety such manuscripts are still extant. But the decision to order the carving of one hundred roof bosses on the theme of the Apocalypse was without parallel. If the theme was suggested by the illuminated manuscripts, the mode of telling the story, through a succession of roof bosses, might have been derived from that first group of five beautiful carvings on Christ's Passion in the east walk.

It is impossible to know what great cycles of carvings have been destroyed over the centuries through the decay of buildings or through vandalism, but in church iconography there are very few examples of a complete representation of the Apocalypse. In the chapter house of Westminster Abbey there were originally a great number of late-fourteenth-century wall-paintings of the Apocalypse. Only a few panels now remain. The great east window of York Minster contains eighty-one lights on the

Apocalypse, the work being undertaken between 1405 and 1408. The Angers Apocalypse tapestry in France, 1375-79, originally contained ninety illustrations. The fifteenth-century rose window of Sainte-Chapelle, Paris, still has its eighty illustrations of the Apocalypse. All offer interesting comparisons with the Norwich cloister bosses, but all post-date the planning and inception of the Norwich work and none is in the medium of stone. Scenes from the Apocalypse were carved in the thirteenth century on the porches of the west front of Rheims Cathedral, again in France, but the work lacks the cyclic scope of that in the Norwich cloisters.

The last book of the Bible, which is ascribed to St John the Divine, was written towards the end of the first century AD in the form of an allegory which foretold the destruction of the wicked, the overthrow of Satan, and the triumph of the new Jerusalem, Christ's kingdom on earth. It was a theme that buoyed up the spirits of the early Christians suffering persecution under the Roman empire. Nero, Domitian, and other oppressive tyrants were readily cast in the role of the Beast or Antichrist. No succeeding age has found difficulty in casting tyrants, or even movements, for the part of the Beast. At the Reformation, for the Catholics the Beast was Protestantism, and for the Protestants it was Papal corruption. The seven deadly sins in the Apocalypse imagery are materialised in the Beast's seven heads. The four creatures about God's throne, lion, ox, man, eagle, became later the symbols of the four Evangelists. The primary conflict of good and evil, illustrated so abundantly in the Middle Ages, in the fall of Man and his redemption through Christ's Passion, in sermon, in art, and in drama, was reinforced by the depiction of the Apocalypse. The scope of the Apocalypse carving in the south walk extends from St John's vision on the isle of Patmos to the War in Heaven, in which Michael and his fellow angels drive Satan and his confederates to hell. The subjects for the carvings in the south walk are derived from Chapters 1 to 12 of the Book of Revelation. The subjects in the west walk are derived from Chapters 12 to 21 and conclude with the blessed being received into heaven and the wicked being cast into the mouth of hell.

overleaf
God blessing his Creation (NA4)

'And God blessed them, saying, Be fruitful, and multiply, and fill the waters in the seas, and let fowl multiply in the earth … And God saw everything that he had made, and, behold, it was very good.'
Genesis 1. 22 and 1. 31.

The bosses in the easternmost bay of the nave deal with the creation of the world. The fourth boss shows God blessing his creation. God has golden hair and beard. He is wearing a full red gown on which are circles of gold outlined with black. The gown has a wide golden border and golden cuffs. God's right hand is raised in benediction. His left hand holds the top of a pair of dividers with which he has just measured out the universe. He is flanked by a crouching lion and a unicorn. Such grouping symbolizes the Trinity. The background is of gold and green foliage.

39

previous page
Noah building the ark (NB4)

Noah wears a long gown decorated with
large green circular patches. His cuffs, the
border of his gown and his belt are
golden; his hose is green and his boots
red. His green hat is held in position by
a golden band. It is probable that the
colours used in the repainting of these
nave bosses in 1938 followed those discovered and recorded by Dean Goulburn in
the 1870s. The part-finished ark rests on a
shelf at the level of Noah's head while he
is planing a plank of wood wedged in position. At his feet are other planks waiting
to be similarly treated. A stone carving on
the west front of Wells Cathedral (*c*.1230)
shows Noah at the same stage of his ark-
building.

The communar and pitancer rolls, part of the medieval records of Norwich Priory, reveal that in the rebuilding of the cloisters, stone from Caen
in Normandy, France, and Purbeck marble from Corfe in Dorset, are
shipped to Norwich. Barnack stone, too, is shipped from the quarries
near Stamford, Lincolnshire. As mentioned earlier, Caen and Barnack
stone had been used when work on the cathedral started. Payments are
recorded to masons and their men, some of whom are named: Richard
Hall, John Ramsey and his nephews, John and William Ramsey; Simon
Hue, a carver; John Attegrene; James and John Woderove. Master masons
received annually, apart from their pay, a furred gown, gloves, and a tunic.
John Horne in 1427-8 was paid as a stone carver 4 shillings (20 pence)
a week for fifteen weeks, and William Reppys carved six keystones for
6s. 8d. each (33 pence). A centre ridge boss took about two weeks to carve.
We learn that in 1346 the masons asked the Priory to supply them with
'A History of the Apocalypse'. The Apocalypse carving was well in hand
at this stage. Perhaps their earlier models, no doubt copied from an earlier
manuscript, had become too thumb-marked to be of further use. An
illuminated manuscript of the Apocalypse would have been too precious
for the prior to allow it to be housed in the masons' workshop but the
master mason might have used it as a basis for his models.

The creation of the great Apocalypse cycle in the south and west walks
was such an innovation that the work must have been admired far and
wide and given the carvers confidence in their prowess and invention for
them to achieve almost as great a sculptural feat in their treatment of the
north walk vaulting. The post-Resurrection themes at the east end of this
walk are closely linked to the first Passion sequence created a hundred
years earlier. Pilate, Caiaphas and Annas sealing Christ's tomb (CNA5
p.25), the three Marys approaching the empty tomb (CNA2), Mary Magdalene meeting the resurrected Christ and thinking him a gardener – he
holds a spade and a pruning knife hangs from his girdle (CNA8), and her
falling down at his feet when he reveals to her the wound in his side (CNB1),
the beautifully carved Supper at Emmaus (CNB5): these are a few of this
third fascinating series which concludes with the death (CNE3) and

coronation (CNE5) of the Virgin Mary. The rest of the walk is devoted to carvings of the saints and martyrs. Foliate and animal themes are now rare. The figured work depicts the saint at his most characteristic moment: St Martin on horseback cutting his cloak with his sword to give half of it to a peasant (CNJ3); St Laurence being roasted on his gridiron (CNI5); St Edward at mass (CNI3); St Clement wearing his papal tiara, cast overboard to drown with an anchor tied to his neck (CNF8). Often only one boss tells the story of the saint, sometimes two as in the cases of St Clement and St Denis (CNI2, CNJ7). For the story of Thomas of Canterbury five carvings mark the different stages (CNH3, CNH5, CNH8, CNI1, CNH6), ending with the remarkable image of Henry II kneeling almost naked at the shrine of the saint, his courtiers to the left hold his clothes, his crown is laid on the ground in front of him, while three monks lean over the shrine and beat him with scourges.

The cloister bosses are of course more subject to weathering than those within the cathedral. There was a major repainting campaign in the 1930s under the direction of Professor Tristram of the Royal College of Art, London. The east and south walks were again cleaned, repaired and repainted in 1989-91. Before further repair and repainting was carried out on the west and north walks the Dean and Chapter were advised by a report from the Courtauld Institute that closer attention might be given to preserving the palette used by Professor Tristram, who more accurately recreated the medieval mode and preserved the earlier subtleties. The report recommended cleaning rather than repainting, and emphasised how the application of a lime wash to the webbing would assist in highlighting the carving. The bay in the north walk containing the bosses concerned with St Thomas of Canterbury has received this sort of treatment. The result is satisfactory and contrasts with the less discriminating painting of, say, the Apocalypse bosses in the south walk.

The main building work in the cloisters came to an end c.1430. The paving of the west walk was not undertaken until 1450-53. This was during the episcopate of Bishop Lyhart (1446-72). In 1463 when fire destroyed the wooden roof of the nave it was Lyhart who planned, and probably

overleaf
Noah's Ark (NB11)

Noah's ark is carved between the water and the sky. It is battlemented fore and aft, and has three decks. Noah and his family and the creatures in the ark look out to sea. At the top level there are three sections. On the left are two squabbling monkeys, in the centre are nine long-beaked birds, and on the right – not seen in this angled shot from the clerestory – is the head of an elephant. At the middle level there are four sections: on the left another group of birds, then Noah and his wife, one of Noah's sons and the son's wife, and on the extreme right – not seen here – the head of a unicorn. Legend maintains that the unicorn was too proud to enter the ark and so is now extinct. The Norwich mason who carved the unicorn at God's right hand (NB4 p.41) was keen to ensure his survival on the ark. At the lowest level there are three compartments: on the left a muzzled bear – a familiar sight at the Tombland bear-baitings; in the centre a cow is on either side of a bull; on the right is a lion.

It is questioned whether these bosses were completed in the masons' workshop and then lowered into position rather than carved on scaffolding *in situ*. Here the treatment of the sky and the sea carved deeply into the groins of the ribs indicates that at least that part of the work must have been completed *in situ*.

Cloister south walk

previous page
Carrying the animals into the ark (NB8)

The centre boss in this bay is a carving showing Noah and his family in the ark, humans and animals looking out to sea. In the surrounding bosses are shown carvings of the embarking and disembarking with the animals, the raven staying to gorge it-self on a carrion horse which has drowned in the flood, and the dove returning with the olive branch in its beak. Here one of Noah's sons carries into the ark a white ewe with gold spots which he holds securely with his right arm, and a ram which he has over his left shoulder.

largely paid for, the new stone vaulting. The great sequences of narrative carving in the cloisters must have considerably influenced the bishop in deciding to span the fourteen-bay vault with the history of the world from the Creation to the Last Judgement.

overleaf **Woman carrying birds into the ark** (NB13)

One of Noah's daughters-in-law carries a basket on her head. The woman sup-ports the basket by its handles which protrude on either side. A group of baby chicks peers out from beneath the lid of the basket. She is taking them into the ark which is carved on the neighbouring boss. She has bare feet and her skirt is hitched up into her girdle as though she has to walk through water.

This image, apart from its association with Noah's ark, might represent a Nor-wich woman in the 1460s bringing her birds to sell in the market, perhaps even in the nave of the cathedral, which at times was used for such purposes.

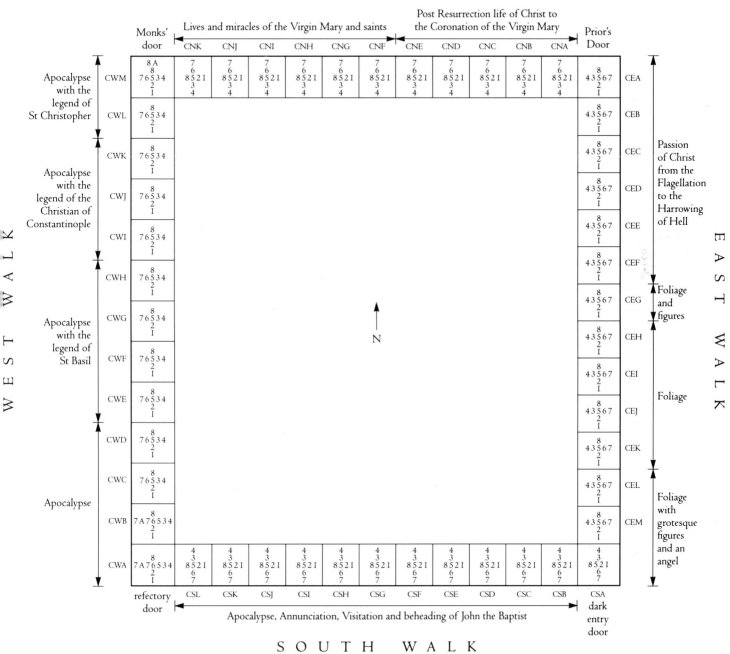

N O R T H   W A L K

Lives and miracles of the Virgin Mary and saints | Post Resurrection life of Christ to the Coronation of the Virgin Mary

Monks' door

CNK CNJ CNI CNH CNG CNF CNE CND CNC CNB CNA

Prior's Door

Apocalypse with the legend of St Christopher — CWM

Apocalypse with the legend of the Christian of Constantinople — CWK CWJ CWI

Apocalypse with the legend of St Basil — CWH CWG CWF CWE

Apocalypse — CWD CWC CWB CWA

CEA CEB CEC CED CEE CEF CEG CEH CEI CEJ CEK CEL CEM

Passion of Christ from the Flagellation to the Harrowing of Hell

Foliage and figures

Foliage

Foliage with grotesque figures and an angel

W E S T   W A L K

E A S T   W A L K

N

refectory door

CSL CSK CSJ CSI CSH CSG CSF CSE CSD CSC CSB CSA dark entry door

Apocalypse, Annunciation, Visitation and beheading of John the Baptist

S O U T H   W A L K

Cloister plan showing iconography of the main series of bosses

previous page
Noah's vineyard (NB18)

'And Noah began to be an husbandman, and planted a vineyard: and he drank of the wine, and was drunken; and he was uncovered in his tent.'

Genesis 9. 20, 21.

Here is Noah planting his vineyard. In another boss within the bay is shown Noah's son and grandson, Ham and Canaan, exposing Noah's nakedness, a prefiguring of the mocking of Christ. Noah has thrust a dibble in the ground and is about to plant a young vine. The rest of his vineyard flourishes with vine-leaves, with an interesting spiral above Noah's head, and many bunches of grapes. Noah, elaborately costumed, has tucked up the front of his gown, which has a green lining, into his girdle to facilitate his work.

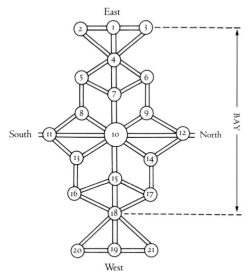

above Nave vault. Location of bosses within the last bay. This plan should be read as if viewed from below.
right The nave vault

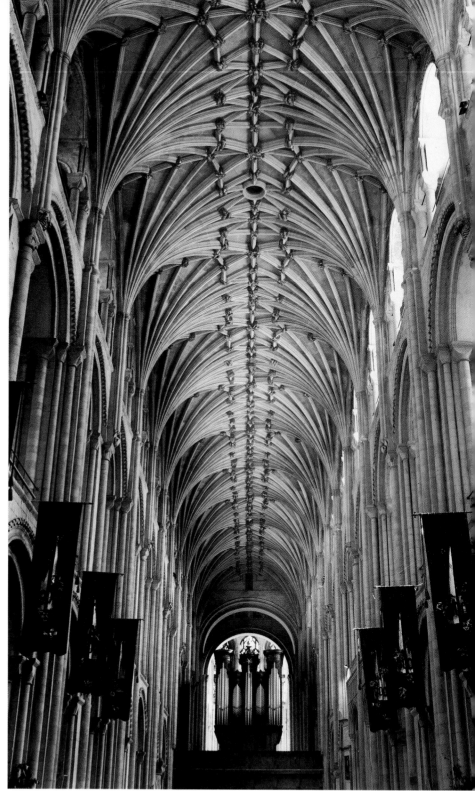

The Nave Roof Bosses

overleaf
Abraham about to sacrifice his son, Isaac (NC10)

This is the centre boss of the third bay whose theme is the story of Abraham and Isaac. God, to test Abraham's obedience, has commanded Abraham to take his son, Isaac, to the land of Moriah, 'and to offer him there on one of the mountains as a burnt offering' (Genesis 22. 2). Abraham, Isaac and a servant make the journey. Isaac is ignorant of its precise purpose but Abraham asks him to carry the wood for the burnt offering. As Christ carries his cross to Calvary so Isaac, unwittingly, carries the wood for his own sacrifice. This prefiguring is seen in an adjacent boss (NC8). In the carving illustrated here Abraham stands over his son with his sword raised. Isaac sits on the altar with his hands held together in prayer. The angel will come in the nick of time to stay Abraham's hand and a ram caught in a thicket (ND3) will be sacrificed instead.

E DWARD IV was crowned king in June 1461. The sun was rising on the house of York. The Lancastrian king, Henry VI, his warlike queen, Margaret, and their young son, Edward, had sought refuge in Scotland. Loyalties among the great Norfolk families were divided. The Duke of Suffolk had fought to maintain the supremacy of the house of Lancaster; the Duke of Norfolk inclined to the house of York. The satellite families followed their respective overlords. When in 1463 the damaged nave roof of the cathedral was in need of extensive repairs the bishop, Walter Lyhart, was called on to take decisive action. Lyhart had previously been chaplain to William de la Pole, then Earl of Suffolk, and also confessor to Queen Margaret. As bishop he was employed abroad to negotiate between contending popes. He had been well rewarded and held many benefices as well as the mastership of St Anthony's hospital in London and university offices at the Oxford colleges of Exeter and Oriel.

He employed his diplomacy and wealth in the early years of the Yorkist's reign to rebuild significant parts of Norwich Cathedral: the tower was restored; the floor of the nave paved; a monument erected over the grave of the founder; a choir screen (pulpitum) erected; and, most splendidly, stone vaulting was built over the fourteen bays of the nave.

His great building undertakings, especially the vaulting, may not have been completed before his death in 1472 in which case it would have been his successor, Bishop Goldwell, who saw the work through. The vaulting springs from the highest point of the Romanesque clerestory windows towards the central longitudinal ridge rib. These ribs, tiercerons, are intersected by shorter ribs, liernes, which form a stellar pattern around the

previous page
Abraham's angel (NCII)

'And the Lord appeared unto him by the oaks of Mamre, as he sat in the tent door in the heat of the day; and he lift up his eyes and looked, and lo, three men stood over against him; and when he saw them, he ran to meet them from the tent door, and bowed himself to the earth …'

Genesis 18. 1, 2.

Norwich Cathedral is consecrated in the name of the Holy and Undivided Trinity. A nave boss at the very west end of the vaulting depicts the Trinity. The passage in Genesis in which God sends three men or angels to visit Abraham and tell him that, though he and his wife, Sarah, are stricken in years, she will yet give birth to a son, was perceived, iconographically, as prefiguring the part played by the Holy Trinity in bringing about the redemption of mankind.

The centre boss of this third bay shows Abraham about to sacrifice Isaac. The satellite bosses graphically explore the story of Abraham. His entertainment of the three angels is shown in three carvings (NC7, NCII, NCI2). They do not sit together but at separate tables. In one of the carvings Abraham stands, waiting on the angel (Gen. 18. 8). Here the angel with spread wings and wearing a cape, has a tiara on his head. On the table before him is spread bread, half a cheese, a capon, a covered dish of salt and a knife.

bay's central boss. The system is known as lierne vaulting: the liernes are more decorative than structural. Similar vaulting is to be seen in the earliest chapels built on the north side of King's College Chapel, Cambridge, the work of Reginald Ely from Coltishall in Norfolk. He received a royal commission in 1443 to design and construct the chapel and he remained in charge until 1461 when Henry VI, the founder of King's College, was deposed and supplanted by Edward IV. It is probable that Ely's earliest design for the vaulting in the chapel at King's was of a lierne style, requiring a multiplicity of roof bosses in each bay, such as was placed in the late 1460s above the nave of Norwich Cathedral. In King's College Chapel the pear-shaped mouldings over the doorway on the south side of the chancel compare with the mouldings over the arch of the Norwich pulpitum, and it could well be that when work in Cambridge came to an abrupt end in 1461, Reginald Ely moved back to Norfolk and was given the job of designing the vaulting for the nave. He died in 1471 and Robert Everard was the mason responsible for the completion of the work on the nave vaulting.

The Cathedral in 1463 was different in many ways from that of 1144 when it was first completed. The main innovations were the very large Early English Lady Chapel built c.1250 at the eastern end, replacing a much smaller apsidal chapel. Two more chapels had been added after the reconstruction following the 1272 riots; St Anne's (the mother of the Virgin Mary) to the north of the ambulatory, and the chapel to Our Lady of Pity to the south of the ambulatory, both c.1329. These three chapels, all associated with the Virgin Mary, were constructed in a period when devotion to the Virgin was growing in popularity. The splendid Lady Chapel at Ely Cathedral c.1321-49 also testifies to such devotion. The iconography within the Norwich chapels, as at Ely, would have corresponded with the dedication. In wood, stone, and paint the imagery must have reflected this fervent veneration of the mother of Christ. Bishop Lyhart would have wished to create story material in the pattern of roof bosses in the nave vault that was complementary to what was to be seen elsewhere in the cathedral. This might account for there being no treatment of the death, assumption and coronation of the Virgin there.

The choice of theme for the carving of the nave vault roof bosses closely resembles that of the stained glass windows in King's College Chapel which are dated 1513-47. Bishop Richard Fox of Winchester (1501-29) was appointed to advise on the form the iconography should take at King's and he chose the theme of the history of the world told through illustration of the Old and New Testaments.

It might be speculated that Reginald Ely had originally planned such a decorative sequence as roof bosses for the chapel but when he moved to Norwich he took his plans with him and offered them as the decorative scheme for the great new nave vaulting there. No doubt Bishop Fox had access to Ely's earlier plans for the King's roof bosses but used them instead for the stained glass windows.

Although, in general, the themes of the King's windows and the Norwich vaulting are similar, the treatment, as well as the medium employed, is different. The essential pattern of the windows is to juxtapose the Old Testament story with the New Testament analogy: for instance in the third window, counting from the north-west, the left-side upper light shows the temptation of Eve, and the lower light the Annunciation; on the right hand side is Moses confronted by the burning bush, and below the scene of the Nativity. The Old Testament story, the 'type', is fulfilled in the New Testament story, 'the anti-type'. Eve in her disobedience to God's commands tastes of the forbidden fruit and persuades Adam to do the same, thus precipitating the fall of man. The Virgin Mary, in her obedience to God's word, enables the redemption of mankind to take place. God appears to Moses in the burning bush and Moses is not consumed by the fire, the type; the Holy Spirit enters the Virgin Mary and she too is not consumed with fire, the anti-type. And so the story of the windows progresses from the north-west to the south-west of King's College Chapel. In the Norwich Cathedral nave vaulting the stories of the Old and New Testaments are not juxtaposed. The two Testaments are separated: the Old appearing in the first seven bays from the east; and the New in the second set of seven bays to the west.

overleaf
Isaac, Esau, and Jacob (NC15)

'And Isaac said unto Jacob, Come near me, I pray thee, that I may feel thee, my son, whether thou be my very son, Esau, or not. And Jacob went near unto Isaac his father; and he felt him, and said, The voice is the voice of Jacob, but the hands are the hands of Esau.'

Genesis 27. 21, 22.

Jacob deceives his blind father, Isaac, by pretending to be his elder twin, Esau, so that he can receive the blessing given to the firstborn. With the aid of his mother, Rebekah, he puts the 'skin of the kids of the goats upon his hands, and upon the smooth of his neck'. Esau is a hairy man; Jacob is a smooth man. The disguising of Jacob is seen in a nearby boss (NC5) in which Rebekah appears to be fitting a beard to Jacob's chin. But in this boss the hairiness of neither Esau nor Jacob is apparent. Esau with his bow in his right hand leaves Isaac's bedside to hunt for the venison which is his father's favourite dish. As he leaves Jacob comes to the bedside to perpetrate his deceit and gain his father's blessing. Isaac, with his eyes almost closed, giving the impression of blindness, lies in bed holding Jacob's right hand. His head rests on a red tasselled pillow. On the bed is a white frilled coverlet.

previous page
Jacob journeys to Paddan-aram (ND4)

'And Isaac sent away Jacob: and he went to Paddan-aram unto Laban, son of Bethuel the Syrian, the brother of Rebekah, Jacob's and Esau's mother.'

Genesis 28. 5.

Esau, cheated of his father's blessing, plans to kill Jacob. Jacob's mother devises that Isaac should send Jacob away for safety to her kin in Paddan-aram. Jacob's staff, prominent in this boss, is a symbol of his travelling and also of the stock that flows from him. It is Jacob who will be called Israel, from whom the twelve tribes stem. Jacob who is richly arrayed stands clutching a large red staff against a background of foliage.

The lierne vaulting of the nave required twenty-four bosses in each of the fourteen bays. In the very last bay by the west window there are an extra three keystones. Another unusual characteristic of this western bay is the way it is raised an additional 4 feet (1.20m) to meet the apex of the great west window which had been inserted only a few years before the new vaulting. In each bay the central boss is larger than the rest, measuring approximately 24 inches (60cm) in diameter. The satellite bosses vary from approximately 10 inches (25cm) to 20 inches (50cm).

Was it possible that this intricate pattern of lierne vaulting extending over the entire nave, requiring three hundred and thirty-nine keystones, might have been planned as a structural entity without detailed consideration being given to the subject of the carving on the bosses? The building of great churches and cathedrals in the Middle Ages was planned as an entity: all parts were knit together and the decorative element was an integral part of the theology informing the whole structure. When in Norwich the nave received for the first time a great stone vault, the stories displayed in the carvings of that vault would be theologically appropriate for that particular part of the cathedral.

The fourteen Norman bays of the nave directed the approach of bishop and master mason; twice seven settled the formula. Groupings of seven had a powerful and mystical hold on the medieval mind. Examples abound: the seven deadly sins; the seven acts of mercy; the seven planets; the seven days of creation; the seven gifts of the Holy Ghost; the seven penitential psalms; the seven sorrows of the Virgin Mary. The list seems endless. Already in the cloisters was a great story cycle carved on the theme of the Apocalypse in which there were depicted the breaking of the seven seals, the sounding of the seven trumpets, and the pouring of the seven vials. The story of the world was therefore going to be told by dividing the fourteen bays into two groups of seven: in the first group, beginning at the eastern end above the choir, was to be told the story of the creation of the world until the coming of Christ; and the second group was to tell the story of Christ's life, death, and Resurrection and end with the Last Judgement.

Taken bay by bay the subjects of the first seven bays are: the creation of the world and the fall of Adam and Eve, Noah and the flood, Abraham and Isaac, Jacob, Joseph, Moses, David. The subjects of the New Testament bays are: the Nativity, the Baptism, the Last Supper, Christ's arrest, the Crucifixion, the Ascension, the Last Judgement.

In each bay the central boss establishes the main subject and the seventeen satellite bosses contribute to the story. Although in each bay there are twenty-four bosses, the three each side at the extreme of the transverse rib are carved with foliate or floral designs. It is the other eighteen that, with few exceptions, illustrate the main theme of the bay, which is announced by the larger central boss. The scheme for the stained glass windows in King's College Chapel had used corresponding subjects from the Old and New Testaments and placed them in the upper and lower register of the same window. In the Norwich vaulting the Testaments are confined to their particular seven bays but within that pattern there are echoes of the type/antitype apparent in the King's College Chapel windows: Noah's Ark in the second bay is a type of Christ's Baptism in the ninth; Solomon sitting in judgement in bay seven is a type of Christ enthroned at the Last Judgement in bay fourteen.

The iconography used both in the Norwich vaulting and in the stained glass windows of King's College Chapel is derived from a variety of much earlier medieval sources, prominent among which is the thirteenth-century *Biblia Pauperum* and the fourteenth-century *Speculum Humanae Salvationis*, instructional picture books in which the types of the Old Testament prefigure the antitypes of the New.

The *Biblia Pauperum* (The Bible of the Poor), and the *Speculum Humanae Salvationis* (The Mirror of Man's Salvation), were probably to be found throughout Europe in workshops associated with major ecclesiastical building projects. The *Biblia Pauperum* is essentially a picture-book presenting on each page, in the centre, a scene from the New Testament, and on either side a scene from the Old Testament. An accompanying Latin text above and below describes the pictures and draws the analogies. The book is learned and sophisticated and rather beyond the grasp of an

overleaf
Jacob wrestles with an angel (ND7)

'And Jacob was left alone; and there wrestled a man with him until the breaking of the day.'

Genesis 32. 24.

This wrestling match comes at the most critical moment of Jacob's career. He struggles with the angel until the angel concedes '... thou hast striven with God and with men and hast prevailed.' And it is from this moment that Jacob's name is changed to Israel, because from him will spring the twelve tribes of a new nation. The wrestling also prefigures Christ's agony in the garden as his human and divine nature come into conflict as he anticipates his fate on Calvary.
The wrestling match seems strangely static but it reflects a medieval mode of wrestling in which the contestants wear special collars of rope or of chain. One hand grasps the opponent's collar and the other hand seeks to ease the pressure placed on one's own collar by the opponent. A misericord in Norwich Cathedral and a roof boss in the cloisters (CWA3) illustrate this mode more graphically. Both Jacob and the angel are bare-foot. It is important for the angel to show his bare feet because devils often disguise themselves as angels but cannot conceal their cloven hoofs. When at the end of *Othello* the Moor recognizes Iago for the devil he is he says 'I look down towards his feet; but that's a fable.' (V.ii.286)

previous page
Jacob peeling his rods (ND10)

'And Jacob took him rods of fresh poplar, and of the almond and of the plane tree; and peeled white strakes in them, and made the white appear which was in the rods.'

Genesis 30. 37.

This is the centre boss in the fourth bay. It shows Jacob peeling his rods. He will then set the rods in the water troughs before the sturdier members of his flocks of sheep and goats when they come to drink at mating time. Their progeny will then be ringstraked, speckled, or spotted, and as such will be Jacob's property and not his uncle, Laban's.
Jacob sits by the river which flows either side of him. He holds a rod in one hand and a knife in the other. The sheep and goats are mating on both banks of the river.
In the Middle Ages Christians were forbidden to practise usury. This was allowed the Jews, who were forbidden any other occupation, and they were given the protection of the king who frequently looked to them for large loans. This story of Jacob's cunning increase of his wealth was an example held by the Jews of God's sanction of usury. And as such it is retold in detail by Shylock in *The Merchant of Venice* (I.iii.72-91)

unlettered 'poor man'. The *Speculum* is similar in intention but it contains three Old Law analogies to set against the one illustration of the New Law, and the accompanying text is very much more detailed. Both books take up strongly the recurring theme in the Bible that 'what has been foretold of old' will now be fulfilled. In the early Middle Ages the Old Testament came to be considered as primarily a prefiguration of what was written in the New Testament, and was as such freely and allegorically interpreted. A great many copies were made of these two books. Perhaps before work was completed on the nave vaulting a printed copy of the *Speculum* from abroad might have been available in the Norwich workshop.

The *Biblia Pauperum* and the *Speculum* were not the only sources that the masons had as their models. As mentioned earlier, when the cloister bosses were being carved, the masons asked for a 'history of the Apocalypse'. Illuminated manuscripts: Bibles, psalters, books of hours, service books, might all furnish them with images from which to model their narrative carvings. And the master masons themselves, like the senior churchmen who consulted them on such matters, were widely travelled and experienced in work in other areas, at home and abroad. Westminster Abbey, York and Lincoln minsters, the great abbey of Bury St Edmunds, Ely and Canterbury cathedrals were all magnificent ecclesiastical centres where the range of iconography introduced into the nave of Norwich Cathedral was already a familiar currency. We know for instance that while the Norwich cloisters were in their early stage of construction the Bishop of Winchester especially asked the Bishop of Norwich to allow a carpenter from Blofield in Norfolk to complete the work on the choir stalls in Winchester Cathedral (1308). There are features of the choir stalls which are similar to some of the Norwich cloister carvings. John Attegrene of Tasburgh, Norfolk, working on the south walk in 1336 was to become master mason at Ely Cathedral and responsible for the building of its remarkable octagon tower. He subsequently became master mason of the King's Works. James Woderove, a Norwich master mason who was responsible with his brother, John, for completing the work on the cloisters and who, John Harvey believes, designed the Erpingham Gate and remodelled the west front of the cathedral, was invited to visit Eton to be consulted on the erection of the new chapel. This was founded by Henry VI in 1440, a year before he granted the first statutes to King's College, Cambridge. In the 1460s there were striking similarities in some features in both King's College Chapel and Norwich Cathedral; in the 1470-80 period there appeared a remarkable correspondence between the murals in the chapel of Eton College and the theme of the roof bosses in the Bauchun Chapel of Norwich Cathedral. The freemasonry of the builder's craft, comprehending both structure and decoration as an integral unity, was widespread in medieval times throughout western Europe.

A marked characteristic of the cloister roof bosses, especially in the early phases, is the profusion of foliate carving. Later, in the cloister areas where Bible stories are depicted they also include a strong foliate element. And alongside such carving are subjects with no relevance to Holy Writ: Green Men, dragons, griffins, hybrids, a wide range of animals, and folk scenes. The treatment of subject material in the nave vault is distinctly different. No Green Man is carved in stone in the nave vault, but there are two Green Men among the misericords in the choir stalls, c.1480. By the mid- to late-fifteenth century they have been confined to areas not generally scrutinized, as though suppressed by the Christian story which has made itself manifest elsewhere. There are no hybrids, monsters or folk scenes in the nave vault. The many creatures, real and imaginary, are carved within the context of the Bible story being told: griffin, unicorn, lion, hart, monkey, eagle, swan. Such creatures also appear at the beginning of many medieval illuminated manuscripts, bibles and psalters, illustrating God's first creation. Elsewhere horses and camels appear in the care of Abraham's servant who goes to find a wife for Isaac; and Mary in her flight into Egypt rides side-saddle on a grey palfrey, clasping her young son in her arms.

The focus of the carving is concentrated on the Bible story and is not diverted by other themes. But it is not the whole of the Bible story that is told. A selection is made which closely matches the range of biblical

overleaf

The flight of Jacob's wives (ND17)

'The Jacob rose up, and set his sons and wives upon camels ...'

Genesis 31. 17.

Laban looks darkly on Jacob because of his greatly increased wealth. Jacob decides to return with his wives, family and possessions to the land of Canaan. He braces himself to meet there his brother, Esau. The mason has placed the two wives of Jacob on horses not camels. They ride side-saddle, holding their swaddled babies in their arms. A green sward forms the background with a hint of foliage.

63

previous page
The marriage of Jacob and Rachel (NDII)

Jacob made a compact with his uncle, Laban, that if he served him for seven years he would be given his daughter, Rachel, in marriage. He is tricked and finds himself married to Leah, the first-born, instead. He promises to serve another seven years for Rachel whom he marries a week after his marriage to Leah. The bosses depicting these two marriages are placed on either side of Jacob peeling his rods (ND10 p.61). In both a priest stands between the pair bringing their right hands together, 'handfasting', that is making the contract of marriage. The priest with crossed stole and maniple over his right wrist is officiating as an ordained Christian priest. The same 'handfasting' is a constant feature of the carvings of the sacrament of marriage on the East Anglian seven sacrament fonts. The font in Norwich Cathedral, which came from a nearby church, shows a similar scene and was carved contemporaneously with these roof bosses. In the marriage of Jacob and Leah (ND12) Jacob is dressed in a plain green gown. In the marriage of Jacob and Rachel (NDII) the bridegroom wears a golden gown and holds in his left hand a large purse.

material used in the medieval mystery plays. The source of such a selection is the Bible readings throughout the Church year; and it is especially those readings, in which the Old Testament reading can clearly be seen to prefigure the New Testament, which find a common place in the picture-books, the mystery plays and the iconography in the vaulting of the nave of Norwich Cathedral. For example, the first lesson on Good Friday relates the story of Abraham, in response to God's command, taking his son Isaac to the land of Moriah to sacrifice him there as a burnt offering (Gen. 22). The second lesson is from John 18 in which Jesus is arrested, led before Pilate, and when the Jews are asked whether they would wish to have Jesus or Barabbas go free, they choose Barabbas. God's command that Abraham should be willing to sacrifice Isaac is paralleled by God's sacrifice of his own son. In the iconography the image of Isaac on his journey with his father to mount Moriah carrying a bundle of kindling wood — and sometimes this is stacked in the shape of a cross — is paralleled by Christ carrying his cross to Calvary. On the Monday of Easter Week the first lesson is from Exodus 15 and tells of the Israelites safely crossing the Red Sea as the waters are rolled back. When Pharaoh and his chariots pursue the Israelites the waters engulf them. The second lesson from Luke 24 tells of Christ's resurrection. As Moses leads his people to the promised land so Christ rises to redeem mankind.

The sacrifice of Isaac/the sacrifice of Christ; the crossing of the Red Sea/the redemption of man through the resurrection — such are the type/antitypes figured in the picture-books and repeated in church iconography throughout western Europe. As mentioned earlier, in the nave vaulting of Norwich Cathedral the type/antitype images are not juxtaposed as in the stained glass of King's College Chapel, but confined to their Old and New Testament bays. For instance, the Abraham and Isaac bosses occur in the third bay and the crucifixion bosses are in the tenth: Pharaoh and his men drowning in the Red Sea is in the sixth bay; the scenes of the resurrection are in the tenth and eleventh bays.

Although the master masons working on the nave vault must have had in their possession versions of the *Biblia Pauperum* and the *Speculum* or were copying work taken from these block books, they were not wholly dependent upon them. They set themselves to follow a very different pattern. They selected their subjects which were prominent in the readings of the festal offices, but the correspondences of type/antitype are not juxtaposed, as in the block books, but separated by the Old and New Testament division of the fourteen bays. The overarching scheme sets out the ages of the world before Christ in the first seven bays: Adam, Noah, Abraham, Jacob, Joseph, Moses, and David, each a type of Christ – leading to the age of Christ, set out in the second set of seven bays, culminating in the end of the world and the last judgement. The patriarchs of the Old Testament, as precursors of Christ, had frequently been represented in medieval art as part of a greater iconographic pattern of Christian theology, as in the east window of York Minster, or the north-east transept window of Canterbury Cathedral, or the sculpted figures in the north porch of Chartres Cathedral, France. Most of the patriarchs also featured as main characters in the section of the mystery plays concerned with the Old Testament. But whereas the mystery plays would have given at least twice as much emphasis to the New Testament as to the Old, the iconography in the nave vaulting is evenly balanced between the two Testaments.

The Bible was not the only source used by pattern-book makers, composers of religious drama, and the church craftsmen. There was a great body of apocryphal material to draw on dealing with the lives of the patriarchs and more particularly the lives of the Virgin Mary, Christ, and the apostles. Such accounts were devotional, embroidered with allegorical significance, and often extensive. The early life of the Virgin Mary, for instance, was extensively treated. In the Norwich vault the story of Cain, featured in two of the roof bosses, shows evidence of an apocryphal source. The biblical story baldly relates that Cain slew Abel for which he is cursed by God, made a fugitive, and a sevenfold curse placed on whoever shall slay him. Lamech, the son of Methushael, intimates to his wives that he has slain Cain and will be cursed 'seventy and sevenfold' (Gen. 4. 24). The images of the two roof bosses show Cain in a bloodstained tunic

overleaf

Joseph put into a pit by his brothers
(NE10)

'And it came to pass, when Joseph was come unto his brethren, that they stript Joseph of his coat, the coat of many colours that was on him; and they took him, and cast him into the pit: and the pit was empty, there was no water in it.'

Genesis 37. 23-24.

Joseph appears with a 'pudding-basin' haircut. He is seen naked from the waist up. The rest of his body is in the pit which has a stone parapet above ground level. A brother on either side is forcing Joseph's head down. The one on the left thrusts with his hand on top of Joseph's head while the one on the right has a staff in his right hand with which to push Joseph down. The foliage in the background is painted red and green. The brothers are fashionably dressed with diapered pleated knee-length tunics and pointed shoes. Each wears a hat with rounded crown and upturned brim. Much of the iconography of the roof bosses in the nave reflects the type/antitype patterning so prevalent in medieval art whereby images of the Old Testament find their echo in those of the New Testament. The image of Joseph in the pit is frequently seen as a type of the New Testament antitype, the entombment of Christ, which in the nave appears seven bays further on in boss NL15.

previous page
Corn in Egypt (NF1)

'And Joseph laid up corn as the sand of the sea, very much, until he left numbering; for it was without number.'

Genesis 41. 49.

Joseph, having interpreted Pharaoh's dreams, is made lord over Egypt, and in the seven years of plenty stores up grain against the lean years.
Joseph stands in his storehouse proprietorially guarding his sacks of grain.

flourishing the jaw-bone of an ass, having just killed Abel; and the death of Cain shows him pierced by an arrow from Lamech's bow. Cain's 'jaw-bone', non-biblical in origin, finds its way into a wide range of medieval iconography and even into the graveyard scene in *Hamlet*. The apocryphal story of the death of Cain is that of a blind archer, Lamech, anxious to maintain his archery skills, asks his boy to align his bow as soon as any game is seen to stir in the undergrowth. At a word from his boy, Lamech lets fly his arrow. He is told that he has accidentally killed Cain. In anger and grief he beats his boy to death with his bow. This is the subject that is treated in the Cain episode in the *N-Town Play*, a mystery cycle of Norfolk provenance; and this is the story that is depicted by the last boss of the first bay in the Norwich nave vault.

The scope of this book does not allow for a detailed treatment of the story material in each of the bays of the nave. An account of the images in two of the bays will be given: one from the Old Testament range and one from the New. The story begins in the first bay west of the crossing. The very first boss represents the first created light in the form of a face of gold from which stem golden rays (NA1). The image might also be interpreted as the sun, created on the fourth day. This boss was put in position when the house of York, led by Edward IV (1461-83, apart from a short period in 1471), was in the ascendant. The 'sun of York' became a favourite emblem of the house of York. It stands at the beginning of the nave vaulting, carrying both religious and dynastic significance. Foliate carvings appear either side of 'the sun' and the following ridge boss is of God blessing the universe he has just created (NA4 p.40). He stands against a background of trees. He wears a long red gown decorated with large circles of gold. His hair is long and golden. He raises his right hand in benediction; in his left hand, by his side, is a pair of dividers, with which the divine architect has just marked out his work. On his right is a unicorn and on his left is a lion. Together they symbolize the Trinity. The birds, beasts, and fishes of creation are seen in the bosses represented by a swan (NA15 p.36), an eagle (NA16 p.37), a hart (NA7), and five fishes including a salmon and a roach (NA17). The hart, which is lying down and is painted white with large circles of gold, has a pair of splendid golden antlers. It is the ridge boss after the carving of God. The bishop responsible for having the nave roof vaulted in stone was Walter Lyhart. On the corbels above the nave piers are carved alternately the bishop's coat of arms, a black bull on a silver shield, and a rebus on his name, a hart lying in a pool of water. Such images are also carved in the roundels on the arch of Lyhart's pulpitum. The image of the hart evokes the first verse of Psalm 42: 'As the hart panteth after the water brooks, so panteth my soul after thee, O God.' In medieval manuscripts depicting the Creation the hart is nearly always to be found among the first created animals. In this first part of the nave vaulting God is seen blessing all the creatures that he has created and by inference Bishop Lyhart as well.

The lion, unicorn, eagle, and swan have noble and royal resonances: the hart no less. It was the symbol chosen by Richard II as his personal emblem. In the late-fourteenth-century altar-piece, the Wilton Diptych (National Gallery, London), even the angels wear the king's badge: a hart lying down, around its neck is a golden crown from which a golden chain is pendent. The nobility of the hart carved in the roof boss, although without golden crown and chain, associates the nobility and piety of the creator of the vaulting with the creator of the universe.

The swan, too, has interesting associations. It is graphically carved and strikingly painted. It is white with gold spots, red bill, and black eyes. It swims in a ripple of water; its wings are half-furled. Around its neck is a coronet. Henry of Lancaster (King Henry IV 1399-1413) married Mary de Bohun in 1380 and used the de Bohun device of the white swan with a golden coronet around its neck as a badge. Later his son, the Prince of Wales, was to use it as a livery badge. It became an emblem closely associated with the house of Lancaster. The building of the nave roof was undertaken during the reign of the Yorkist, King Edward IV (1461-83). There was still a strong faction in East Anglia sympathetic to the Lancastrian cause. Lyhart himself had been confessor to Henry VI's queen and also acted for the king in an ambassadorial role. The first boss had been the sun's face rayed, a Yorkist emblem; the gorged swan a

overleaf
Moses in the bulrushes (NF4)

'… and when she (the mother of Moses) saw him that he was a goodly child, she hid him three months. And when she could not longer hide him, she took for him an ark of bulrushes, and daubed it with slime and with pitch; and she put the child therein, and laid it in the flags by the river's brink.'

Exodus 2. 2, 3.

Moses is being placed by his mother in the ark and put in the river which is coloured green above and blue below. The baby is wrapped in white swaddling clothes held together with red bands. His mother, who bends lovingly over him, has long hair that falls behind nearly to her waist. She is dressed in a golden gown with a white apron tied at the waist. The ark is painted gold and has a brown lid and a brown central strut which passes under the ark and might serve as the fulcrum of a rocking cradle. On top of the ark at either end are two small golden handles for carrying.

71

previous page
The Israelites rejoice at their deliverance from Pharaoh (NF9)

'I will sing unto the Lord, for he hath triumphed gloriously ... Pharaoh's chariots and his host hath he cast into the sea: and his chosen captains are sunk in the Red Sea. The deeps cover them: They went down into the depths like a stone.'

Exodus 15. 1 ... 5.

The Israelites crossed the Red Sea walking on dry land between two great walls of water. When Pharaoh and his chariots pursued them the walls of water engulfed them. Moses sang a song of praise to the Lord; Miriam, Aaron's sister, 'took a timbrel in her hand; and all the women went out after her with timbrels and dances.' In the nave vaulting on either side, close to the spectacular boss of Pharaoh drowning in the Red sea, are carvings of the Israelites rejoicing by playing musical instruments. In one (NF8) a lute and harp are being played by two men. In the illustration shown here the two musicians wear short tunics and red hose. The one to the right wears a cloak and from his trumpet a red cross banner is pendent, giving him the appearance of a herald. The other blows a woodwind instrument, perhaps a shawm. Both musicians have markedly puffed cheeks.

Lancastrian. The masons and perhaps even the bishop were looking both ways.

The large centre boss of the bay is of the temptation of Adam and Eve in the garden of Eden (NA11, front cover). On either side are the creation of Adam (NA12) to the north, and of Eve (NA10) to the south. God, costumed as before in a red robe with circles of gold edged with black, brings forth Adam, clutching him by his right wrist. God is against a background of foliage; Adam against a green sward, as though he is coming from the earth itself. Adam's hair is dark and reaches below his shoulders. Both God's and Adam's beards appear stuck to their lower lips like stage properties. As Adam rises from the ground his face is lifted up and his eyes are wide open as though staring in wonder at this first view of a brave new world.

In the creation of Eve, Adam lies stretched out on the right, fast asleep. God is on the left, and he draws forth Eve by her right hand from a slit in Adam's side. She too looks with wonder at the world, but God's right hand seems to be raised towards her as though in warning.

In the boss representing the temptation of Adam and Eve, the tree of knowledge is covered with pointed green leaves and an abundance of golden apples. The trunk of the tree is set in a round stand which as a prop in a play, might make it readily portable. Satan is disguised: his bottom half is a serpent's tail encircling the tree-trunk; the top half is that of a female with curled hair and small breasts. Satan has an apple in his right hand and is picking another with his left. Eve, too, holds an apple in each hand. The one in the right she offers to Adam. Adam holds an apple in his left hand. He looks at Eve and his face shows shock and dismay. The way in which the apples are placed in the three characters' hands points to this being a carving describing three movements in the one scene: Satan picks an apple and hands it to Eve; Eve receives the apple and hands it to Adam; Adam takes the apple from Eve and realizes what might be the consequences of his action. Such a sequence is seen in the *Holkham Bible Picture Book* (fol. 4).

The last boss in the bay is of the death of Cain. The first boss in the second bay shows Cain holding above his head the jaw-bone of an ass. Chronologically the 'jaw-bone' should come before the 'death', but in the story-patterns worked out by the masons, chronology is not the primary concern. The last boss in each bay is usually larger than those nearest it and is especially striking in its subject matter: Noah planting his vine-yard (NB18 p.49); Samson rending the lion (NF18); Solomon enthroned (NG18 p.80). The last boss in the bay often, in its subject, looks forward to the theme of the next bay. The first bay deals with the fall of man; the second bay with Noah and the flood. God repents that he made man because of the sinfulness of man. Cain, the first murderer, is a pointer to that sinfulness.

The bosses are to be read radially rather than linearly along the ridge boss. It becomes a type of theatre-in-the-round with smaller stages on the periphery: the main action takes place in the centre and announces the main theme. The dramas that precede and follow are told around this central point. The bosses are usually so oriented that the viewer must turn his head to read the satellite bosses but finds that he is nearly always looking towards the central action.

The Old Testament story continues from that of Noah to that of Abra-ham in the third bay, with two separate bosses devoted to Abraham's im-pending sacrifice of Isaac (NC8, NC10 p.52). This is the only example in the vaulting where an event is portrayed twice, albeit the treatment is dif-ferent. The prefiguring of the crucifixion of Christ is thus underlined. Bays devoted to Jacob, Joseph, Moses and David follow. In the seventh bay the centre boss shows the crowning of David (NG10). Zadok the Priest (NG14) and Nathan the Prophet (NG13) are featured nearby. Echoes of this coronation event, to Handelian strains, are still heard at the crowning of the British monarch. On his deathbed David hands over his sceptre to his young son, Solomon (NG15 p.81). The bay marks the lineal descent of Jesus Christ. The next bay tells the story of Christ's Nativity.

The seven bays that deal with the New Testament begin with the birth of Christ and end with the Last Judgement. The five intermediate bays have as their central themes: the Baptism of Christ (NI10); the Last Supper

overleaf
Samson and Delilah (NG3)

'And she made him sleep upon her knees; and she called for a man, and shaved off the seven locks of his head; and she began to afflict him, and his strength went from him.'

Judges 16. 19.

Eve and Delilah are taken as examples of Old Testament women who, being tempted by evil, the serpent on the one hand and Philistines on the other, brought misery to man. By contrast the Virgin Mary, by being obedient to the voice of God, became the instrument whereby mankind was redeemed.

This carving of Samson and Delilah is in the seventh bay of the nave. The carvings in this bay include Samuel carrying off the Gates of Gaza, David overcoming Goliath (NG4 p.77), the crowning of Solomon (NG18 p.80), Nathan the Prophet and Zadok the Priest. These are tantamount to prophetic statements about the coming of Christ, which is the subject of the carv-ings in the next bay.

Delilah sits with Samson's head in her lap. She wears a large horn-shaped headdress, a style often associated with those of the Devil's party. She has a fashionable v-necked gown, and in her hand she holds a pair of spring shears, but they are as large as those used for shearing sheep. She holds in her left hand one of Samson's locks which she is about to cut. He lies asleep. He has long golden hair and a golden beard. His wrists are tied together. Above him on the ledge of the rib rests his very tall red hat with rounded crown and turned-up brim.

previous page
David and Goliath (NG4)

The Norwich Smiths' Guild was assigned the pageant of *The Conflict of David and Goliath* (*c*.1530). It is reasonable to assume that such a pageant had been part of the Norwich plays for the past hundred years. Norwich seems to have the only extant record of a pageant on the theme of David, and it is therefore interesting to note the many roof bosses, in nave and cloisters, devoted to the life and death of David.

The subject of the centre boss of this bay is the Coronation of King David. This is the last of the Old Testament bays and the narrative material of the bosses leads on to the Annunciation and Nativity of Christ.

Here, David as a young boy confronts Goliath. David has swung his sling with his right hand and his pebble is lodged in the middle of Goliath's forehead. David's other pebbles will not be needed. He has them pouched together in the turned-up part of his tunic. Goliath is rocked backwards by the impact of the pebble. The visor of his helmet is raised. He is dressed in full armour which is articulated at each joint. Behind him a battle mace is thrust into the ground. It has a fleur-de-lis pattern at the top and half way down. His great sword with decorated cross-guard and hilt tips is curved as a falchion, a sword shape associated with the infidels who fought against the crusaders.

(NJ10 p.97); Christ before Pilate (NK10 p.101); the Crucifixion (NL10 p.112); and the Ascension (NM10). There is scarcely any treatment of Christ's ministry. This is similar to the selection of themes for the mystery plays. The raising of Lazarus (NI15) is included, as it invariably is in the plays, as prefiguring Christ's own resurrection. But there are significant omissions. There are no bosses covering the death, assumption, and coronation of the Blessed Virgin Mary, subjects found in most iconographic representations of the history of the world. It may be that these themes had been extensively treated in the Lady Chapel, St Anne's Chapel and the Chapel of Our Lady of Pity. Nor is much made of the visit of the shepherds and the Magi in the Nativity sequence. Rather insignificant carvings of the Magi appear on either side of the centre boss which delightfully shows the infant Christ lying naked in the manger flanked by Joseph and Mary. Above and breathing into the manger, to keep the child warm, are the ox and the ass. Small bosses on either side show the Magi: to the north two Magi walk with their offerings (NH12); and to the south one (NH11). Only one boss shows the shepherds (NH14 p.85). There are two shepherds: one, carrying a crook, points upwards as though he has just heard the angel sing '*Gloria in excelsis*'; the other, wearing a high-crowned bowler hat blandly continues with his piping. Two sheep snuggle closely to the shepherds. It is a beautiful and expressive carving, but unusual because it stands alone without this popular theme being more fully developed.

In the whole range of these New Testament carvings there is much work of exquisite quality such as the tying of Christ to the cross (NL4), the Crucifixion (NL10), and the Ascension (NM10). But there is also work of a cruder kind which might point to an apprentice's hand. The scourgers (NK8), the executioners with hammer and nails (NL3), the soldiers, one with an axe and one with an halberd (NL9), and the two soldiers with battle-axes going to break the legs of the crucified thieves (NK14), are all graphic carvings and in their context threatening, but a heaviness and lack of finesse mark them as the work of an inferior craftsman.

This section ends with an account of the fourteenth bay, the Last

Judgement. Scenes of the Last Judgement were frequently painted above the chancel arches in churches, facing west so that the congregation might have a clear and terrifying understanding of what might befall them if they were damned to hell. Sometimes the last judgement was to be the subject of the west windows in churches, as had been planned for King's College Chapel. In Norwich Cathedral the westernmost bay of the vaulting was to carry the message of salvation or damnation through its twenty-one narrative bosses.

The last boss in the preceding bay had shown the coming of the Holy Spirit at Pentecost. The Virgin and the apostles are overshadowed by an enormous dove from whose extended wings golden rays fall on those below. The Holy Spirit confers new powers on the apostles to cast out demons from those who are so possessed (Mark 16. 17). The first three bosses in the fourteenth bay look back to the theme announced by the last boss of the previous bay. We see a demon being cast out of a man's mouth (NN1) and apostles scourging demons with small wings and cloven feet (NN2, NN3). The wings of the demons are scarcely large enough to get them airborne. The whips comprise a stock and three knotted thongs.

The mouth of hell yawns wide ready to receive the evil souls (NN4). It is carved in profile showing a blue-grey skin, a protruding eye, black, red and gold, a small bat-like ear, and wavy golden whiskers. The nose is stubbed and within the gaping jaws, towards the back at the top, are two enormous canine teeth in front of which are seven serviceable incisors. Within the mouth are three damned souls. One has bruise or scratch marks on his body. The damned souls are guarded by a toad-like creature who sits in hell's mouth. His green skin is spotted black.

A number of bosses within the bay show devils driving the damned souls to hell and angels leading the blessed to heaven. An example will be given of each. A grotesque feathered devil carries towards hell two damned souls (NN5). He grips a red-haired victim over his shoulder and carries the other upside down in front of him. The bodies of both his victims are naked and they are covered with bloody scratches. The devil has a red face, a sharp hooked nose, and fierce claws on hands and feet. In contrast

overleaf
King Solomon (NG18)

'Then Solomon sat on the throne of the Lord as king instead of David his father, and prospered; and all Israel obeyed him.'
1 Chronicles 29. 23.

Solomon is seated on a bench-throne grandly arrayed. He wears his crown above a dome-shaped hat and has an ermine tippet and an ermine border to his golden robe. In his right hand he holds the temple that he has built. It is in the form of a cruciform church with central tower, spire, and transepts. The crosses mentioned by Goulburn on each of the gables are no longer there. Is this image of Solomon's temple modelled on Norwich Cathedral as it was restructured in the course of the fifteenth century? In his left hand Solomon holds the sword of state. It is a curious fact that after Henry VIII's break with Rome in the 1530s the king, claiming supreme authority over church and state, should have been depicted as Solomon in one of the stained glass windows in King's College Chapel, Cambridge.

previous page
David and Solomon (NG15)

'Now the days of David drew nigh that he should die; and he charged Solomon his son, saying, I go the way of all the earth: be thou strong therefore, and shew thyself a man; and keep the charge of the Lord thy God.'

1 Kings 2. 1-3.

Before David dies he counsels Solomon concerning friends and foes and as a symbolic act hands over to him his sceptre. Here David is seen lying in bed, presumably naked except for the crown on his head. It is patterned with red-lined strawberry leaves. His beard is forked and flowing. The golden bedclothes have a red border which reaches to David's chest. In his left hand he holds a sceptre and the palm of his right hand is placed on the head of Solomon who stands in the groin of the boss with his right hand on the base of the sceptre. Solomon is dressed in a short tunic drawn in at the waist. His hose and shoes are red.

Dean Goulburn noted in the 1870s that the boss was damaged. Solomon's head was missing, as was David's right hand and the upper end of the sceptre. The repair work has been successfully undertaken.

an angel leads three of the blessed into heaven (NN9). The good souls are two men and a woman. The two men go first: they have short, cropped golden hair; the woman has long golden hair. The angel holds the first man by the right wrist. They all look upwards. The angel is dressed in a long, pleated, golden gown with a high neck-line. It is as though the three blessed souls are being given archangelic treatment.

The centre boss of the bay is of Christ enthroned in judgement (NN10 p.117). Behind him are the eradiating beams of the sun and at his feet is the crescent moon. Christ wears the stigmata. His mantle rests on his shoulders but leaves his torso bare, revealing the wound in his side. On either side, emerging from blue clouds, is an angel blowing a trumpet. Each angel has curly golden hair over which is a skull-cap with upturned brim. In the earth beneath, to the left of Christ, is a coffin from which a naked, pot-bellied, figure is emerging. Its right arm and leg are out of the coffin, but the head is twisted round to look up to Christ with some apprehension. On the head is the triple tiara of a pope. To the right of the judgement seat a figure is seen from the waist upwards. He is naked apart from his tall, jewelled crown. His hands are together in prayer. Above and below the king and the pope the earth has foliage and flowers. The king on the right of the judgement seat will be welcomed into heaven; the pope on the left will be doomed to hell.

Wonderfully carved angels appear on either side of the central boss (NN11, NN12). Peter with his tonsured head holds two giant keys in his left hand (NN15). The wards are level with his face. The clouds of heaven form a background. The Trinity are enthroned on a bench-seat (NN18): God the Father is in the centre, the Holy Ghost similarly dressed is on the right; Christ with a crown of thorns on his head, showing the wound in his side and the stigmata on his hands, is on the left. Each raises his right hand in benediction. The effulgent beams of heaven eradiate behind them. It is fitting that as this great narrative cycle nears its end the dedication of the cathedral is remembered: the Holy and Undivided Trinity.

The very last boss, at the apex of the great west window, is a small carving of a mitred bishop. His hands are held together in prayer holding in place his crozier which passes across his body and over his right shoulder. It is a representation of Walter Lyhart who initiated the work on the stone nave vaulting. Reference to Lyhart is made in the first bay by the carving of a magnificent hart as one of the first created beings. His coat of arms, a black bull on a silver shield, and his rebus a hart lying in a pool of water, appear as corbels above alternate nave columns. Walter Lyhart is firmly identified with the great work he had carried out. He lies buried under his pulpitum: his head to the west and his feet to the east. When the last trump sounds, as he rises to look to the east, he will see once again the vaulting of his nave before he passes on to even greater glory.

overleaf
Pharaoh drowning in the Red Sea (NF10)

This is the most easily identified boss from ground level because of the painting of the Red Sea. It is also the centre boss of the bay and therefore considerably larger than its satellites. The subject is very frequently treated in medieval iconography and is understood as pre-figuring Christ's descent into hell after his death on the cross. This apocryphal episode is called 'The Harrowing of Hell'. Just as God's hand destroyed Pharaoh and his chariots in the Red Sea and allowed the Israelites to pass into the promised land, so Christ goes down to hell, over-comes Satan, and leads out of limbo and into heaven those good souls, which in-clude Adam and Eve and the prophets, who have awaited this moment of redemption.

Within the Norwich cycle of mystery plays there is one assigned to the Tanners and Cordwainers (1530) entitled *Moses and Aaron with the Children of Israel and Pharaoh with his Knights*. In this illustration Pharaoh with his crown and gold-plated armour is dressed as a fifteenth-century king. Three of his 'knights' are seen keeping their heads just above water. On the extreme left is a booted leg. Pharaoh's chariot, perhaps another reflection of the drama of the time, is a farmer's cart.

previous page

Two shepherds of the Nativity (NH14)

The eighth bay of the nave vaulting is
decorated with bosses associated with
Christ's Nativity, one of the most popular
themes in Christian iconography. But,
strangely, here the offering of the shepherds and the Magi are not represented.
The Magi are carved carrying their gifts
on their way to the manger, one by himself to the south (NH11) of the Nativity
and two, walking together, to the north
(NH12). This carving of the shepherds
is the only one to appear in the nave,
although they are so frequently carved in
the north transept. One shepherd plays
on his pipe. The other looks up as though
he has just heard the angel sing '*Gloria in
excelsis deo*'. He points upwards with the
index finger of his right hand. He carries
a crook over his left shoulder, and at his
side hangs a leathern water container.
Sheep are carved close to both shepherds.
Each shepherd has engaging headgear.

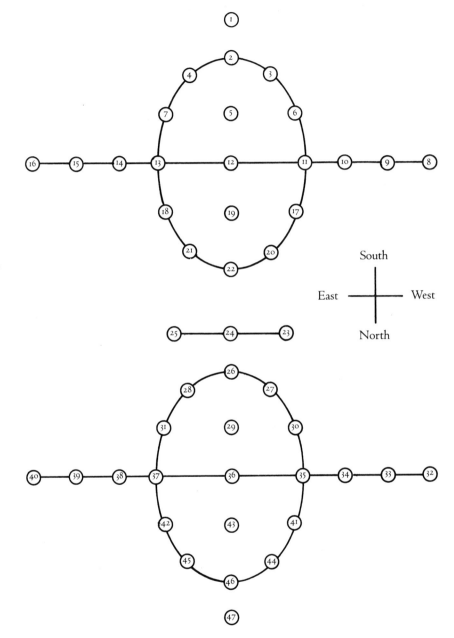

Bauchun Chapel. Location of bosses. This plan should be read as if viewed from below.
The numbering follows that used by M. R. James (1908).

The Bauchun Chapel and the Presbytery

THE BAUCHUN CHAPEL

THE stone vaults were erected in the Bauchun Chapel and the presbytery during the episcopate of James Goldwell (1472-99). Although, roughly speaking, both follow the lierne pattern employed in the nave, the structural function of the vaulting in the two places is fundamentally different, and so is the approach to the subject-matter of the carvings.

The Bauchun Chapel was built in the early part of the fourteenth century. It is named after William Bauchun, a member of the monastic community who acted as *granarius*, the keeper of grain. Money for building the chapel was left in Bauchun's will, and we learn from the communar rolls that the work was in hand in 1327-29. Bauchun's tomb, it is believed, lies beneath the chapel's south window. The lierne vaulting, containing the bosses, was not built until towards the last quarter of the fifteenth century. Another bequest enabled this work to be carried out. William Sekyngton was the benefactor. He had acted as advocate in the consistory court, which had been held in the Bauchun Chapel, and as Corrector of Crimes to Bishop Alnwick (1425-36), who had been particularly zealous in bringing the Lollards to face trials of heresy. Sekyngton died in 1460. It was probably some little time after this, about 1475, that the Bauchun Chapel roof bosses were carved.

On the west wall is a corbel showing William Sekyngton at prayer. His coats of arms are shown upheld by angels on the two south corbels. The shields are damaged and the vestiges of the arms comprising a star

overleaf
The Presentation (NH7)

'And when the days of their purification according to the law of Moses were fulfilled, they brought him up to Jerusalem, to present him to the Lord.'
Luke 2. 22.

This small boss depicts the Presentation of Christ in the Temple rather than the Circumcision. The feast of the Presentation, alternatively called the feast of the Purification of the Virgin Mary, or Candlemas, is kept on 2 February. In images of the Circumcision the priest is usually shown with a small knife in his hand. Also, in the passage from St Luke there is mention of an offering of a pair of turtledoves, or two young pigeons being required. In the neighbouring boss (NH8) Joseph carries an osier basket from which two small doves peep over the edge. Here the Virgin Mary places her naked son upon the altar which is covered by a white cloth edged with gold. On the right a priest, mitred as a bishop, receives the child.

At the end of the play of the *Purification* within the *N-Town Play*, a mystery cycle of Norfolk provenance, the date 1468 appears in the manuscript, a date that must be almost contemporaneous with this carving.

previous page
The Nativity (NH10)

Mary and Joseph sit on either side of the manger in which lies the naked Christ child. Above, the ox and the ass are carved in the ribs' groins. They have their heads over the rim of the manger as though they too have come to adore the infant king. Joseph, like Jacob, is frequently depicted with a red staff. In the Norwich bosses his staff usually has a crook handle. The Virgin Mary wears a patterned cap from which flows her copious hair. Her golden gown is lined with white. The presentation of the richness of the garments worn by Mary and Joseph makes no concession to the reality of their poverty but mirrors the opulence of their images seen in contemporary shrines.

and three chevrons are not easy to distinguish. The chapel is dedicated to Our Lady of Pity. The corbel on the east wall above the recess for the altar depicts a pieta, the Virgin Mary seated with the dead Christ lying across her lap. That the Virgin Mary is especially venerated in this chapel is immediately apparent by a glance at the vaulting where the two most prominent roof bosses are the Assumption (BC12) and Coronation of the Virgin (BC36). The vaulting is divided into two bays. In each bay the bosses are arranged in the form of an ellipse. The centre boss in each bay is of the Virgin, her Assumption to the south and her Coronation to the north. On either side of these central images, east and west, beyond the ellipse on the transverse ribs, are three additional bosses. In all the vaulting contains forty-seven bosses of which most tell the story of the Empress. The arrangement of the bosses is illustrated on page 86.

M. R. James in *The Sculptured Bosses in the Roof of the Bauchun Chapel of Our Lady of Pity*, 1908, declared that the subject of the bosses 'is identical in its main features with Chaucer's *Man of Laws Tale*.' In Chaucer the calumniated lady is an emperor's daughter; in the bosses she is clearly an empress. It is true that Chaucer's Tale and the bosses share as their theme the story of a falsely accused lady of the highest estate, and an incident in which a man, thwarted in his illicit love for the lady, commits a murder and places the incriminating weapon, a dagger, in the hand of the sleeping lady. The folk-lore and literature of the Middle Ages were rich in material relating to falsely accused queens. The Bauchun Chapel bosses and Chaucer's Tale are two such versions but their details, apart from the planted dagger, are fundamentally different.

James identifies the source of the story of the Bauchun Chapel bosses as that of the tale of the calumniated empress to be found in the *Gesta Romanorum*, a collection of stories in Latin compiled in England in the thirteenth century. The Bauchun version, James discovers, is analogous to that told by the fifteenth-century murals found above the south side of the choir in Eton College Chapel. An emperor going to the wars leaves his authority in the hands of his empress. The emperor's brother makes unwelcome overtures of love which the empress firmly rejects. On the emperor's return the brother accuses the empress of licentiousness. She is tried, found guilty and condemned to death, and taken to a forest to be killed. She is rescued by a passing knight who, not knowing that she is an empress, makes her his son's nurse. The knight's brother attempts to seduce her and fails. He takes his revenge by killing his nephew and placing the murder weapon, his dagger, in the hand of the sleeping empress. She is accused of murder and banished. She calls on the Virgin Mary for help and is shown a plant that cures leprosy. She returns to the knight's domain and cures his brother of leprosy. She then returns to where the emperor's brother is also suffering from leprosy, and cures him too. In medieval times it was thought that no medical cure could be effected without the sick person's full confession. And so it is made manifest that the empress has been falsely accused. At this stage she reveals her identity. In the Eton version she takes the veil; in the Bauchun Chapel version she is reconciled to the emperor.

Costume, gesture, and style of the Eton Chapel murals are redolent of the late-fifteenth-century Flemish court. In none of the murals does the Virgin Mary appear. The empress wears her crown throughout except in the last panel when she appears as a nun. The resemblance of the story content to the detail in the Bauchun Chapel bosses is striking, although the style is different. In the Norwich bosses the empress is always recognizable by her triple crown which she wears on all occasions, even as a nurse asleep in bed. Just as in the nave bosses Pharaoh, drowning in the Red Sea, or David, naked in bed giving his charge to Solomon, are recognizable by their crowns, so one can identify the empress, even when some of the characters in the story fail to do so, by her elaborate high crown which mostly overtops the emperor's.

Thirty-five of the forty-seven bosses are devoted to the story of the empress. The other twelve are located on either side of the two central bosses and are of angels holding a cross on which is written *Gaudent Angeli* (the angels rejoice) from the antiphon sung for the Assumption of the Virgin (15 August), and of angels playing musical instruments and rejoicing at the Coronation of the Virgin. The extended story of the

overleaf
Christ and the doctors (N14)

'And it came to pass, after three days, they found him in the temple, sitting in the midst of the doctors, both hearing them and asking them questions.'

Luke 2. 46.

When Christ is twelve years old Mary and Joseph take him to Jerusalem for the Feast of the Passover. On the way home they notice that he is missing from their group. They take three days to find him. Christ as a young boy is seated in a high-backed chair. In his left hand is a closed book. There are three doctors of the Hebrew law: one on either side and one at his feet. Each holds out an open book as though contesting Christ's interpretation of the letter of the law.

previous page
Cana (N17)

This carving in the nave probably represents Christ and his mother at the marriage feast at Cana, although only the two of them are seen seated at the table. Christ wears a robe and girdle. His beard is forked, his hair long. His right hand is on the table, with his left he holds his mother's wrist. Her hair is long and falls over her shoulders. On the table are two small loaves and a chicken in a dish. The probability that this carving is associated with the first miracle is reinforced by there being three amphorae beneath the table and three others in a neighbouring boss where a servant is seen preparing to attend to the feast. The six water-pots are regularly associated with the miracle at Cana: they are likened to the Six Ages of Man.

calumniated empress heralds a new development within the cathedral. The substance of a medieval romance is being used in this Chapel of Our Lady of Pity to engage the attention and interest of the viewers, and to serve as a piece of Christian didacticism. And who *were* the viewers in this chapel which lies to the south of the ambulatory of the presbytery? This was an area largely reserved for the monks themselves, but used on occasion by pilgrims progressing round the ambulatory when visiting the cathedral's holy relics.

The bosses that tell the empress's story are set in no logical sequence. They are scattered haphazardly throughout the two bays. When the roof of the Bauchun Chapel was raised in the fifteenth century as a consequence of Sekyngton's bequest, the vaulting was built of brick. When the chapel was being redecorated in 1966, in preparation for its rededication, it was noticed that only the main ridge stone ribs were integrated with the roof. Therefore as most of the ribs were not essential to the structure of the vault the keystones, or bosses, are decorative rather than functional and would most probably have been carved in the workshop and not *in situ*. It follows that the workmen, ignorant of the correct sequence, might have slotted them in as they came to hand. An apprentice's hand is apparent in much of the carving. The positioning of the bosses might also have been undertaken by an apprentice. But the master mason was not idle the whole time. The two bays' central bosses of the Assumption and Coronation of the Virgin are of high quality, and those of the empress side-saddle on her horse, surrounded by her mounted ladies-in-waiting and by suppliants (BC11, BC35) show a keen sense of composition in which many clearly defined characters are skilfully contained in the bustle of activity within the hemisphere of carving. An example is that of the emperor riding off to war and leaving the empress in charge (BC26). The empress sits side-saddle in the centre of the boss. She wears her triple crown and is dressed in a high-waisted v-necked gown beneath which her bodice is seen. In her left hand she holds the stock of a scourge whose knotted thongs fall downwards over her dress. With her right hand she holds the broad, decorated red and gold headstall of the horse. Bands with tasselled ends fall either side of her saddle. Her horse is in motion with its front feet raised. Behind her to the right are two attendant ladies, also mounted side-saddle. Their gowns have the same cut as the empress's but they wear tall steeple hats with wide decorated frontal bands which, falling down, cover the sides of their heads as lappets. Behind the empress and to the left is the mounted figure of the emperor. His horse with ornamented caparisons is missing its head. The emperor is clearly riding in another direction. His own extended crown stretches across the top of the boss at right angles to the empress's crown. The pommel, hilt, cross-guard and scabbard-top of the emperor's sword are seen hanging by his side. Intriguingly, there is another face to be seen peering straight ahead, between the empress and her first attendant lady. It is as though, as soon as the emperor rides off to the wars his brother is preparing his assault on the empress's virtue.

The quality of the carving is variable: the hands of master mason and apprentice are readily distinguished. Furthermore the repainting of the bosses during the redecorations of 1966, particularly the gold work, lacked finesse. This series of carvings, nevertheless, is unique. Its theme is wholly appropriate for this chapel dedicated to Our Lady of Pity.

overleaf
The feast at Bethany (N118)

'So they made him a supper there: and Martha served … Mary took a pound of ointment of spikenard, very precious, and anointed the feet of Jesus, and wiped his feet with her hair: and the house was filled with the odour of the ointment.'

St John 12. 2, 3.

Christ sits at the table and Martha, waiting on him, offers a flagon of wine. On the table is a chicken on a plate, a dish of salt, a loaf of bread, a cheese(?), and a knife. Beneath the table is a large sealed jar of wine. Also stretched out beneath the table is Mary, with her hair streaming down her back, administering to Christ's feet.

THE PRESBYTERY

In 1362 a violent storm brought the cathedral spire crashing through the presbytery roof, greatly damaging the Norman clerestory. The subsequent rebuilding, undertaken during the episcopate of Thomas Percy (1355-69), created an elegant and much lighter clerestory. The very much larger windows with their stone tracery were built in a transitional style of late Decorated and early Perpendicular. It was not, however, until a century later that the stellar lierne vaulting was added. The fire of 1463 that destroyed the roofing of the nave also caused extensive damage to the presbytery. Traces of that damage are still to be seen in the reddish tinge

Numbering system for the Presbytery

There are one hundred and twenty-eight roof bosses in the vaulting of the presbytery. For the purposes of identification the numbering 1-128 begins at the west end and finishes at the east end of the apsidal vaulting. References to particular presbytery bosses have the letter P followed by the number of the boss.

previous page
The Last Supper (NJ10)

Christ and eight disciples are seated on bench seats around a rectangular table. Christ has his left arm over John's head which rests on the edge of the table. Christ's right hand is on a golden dish which contains two large fish. At the back of Christ's head is a spangled halo. On Christ's right is the tonsured Peter, holding a large key in both hands. Another disciple sits next to Peter and three others sit opposite. The one holding a bowl is missing his head. The one in the middle has his right hand on a small loaf of bread. At the ends of the table, on the left-hand side sits a disciple (Bartholomew?) with his left hand on a large red-handled knife, and on the right James the Greater who holds a flagon with both hands. Attached to his back is his pilgrim's hat; a scalloped shell is attached to his right shoulder.

There are frequent representations of the Last Supper with less than twelve disciples, and often fish rather than lamb is depicted as the main dish. In the east window of the Great Malvern Priory Church there is a stained glass representation of the Last Supper, completed about 1440, showing Christ with eight disciples. On the table is a large golden dish containing two fish.

In medieval iconography Peter often appears with a tonsure, as though he has commenced his ministry at the Last Supper, after Christ has washed his feet. The *Holkham Bible Picture Book* (f.28), *c.*1330, offers such an example.

left on some of the Caen stonework. The vaulting of the presbytery was undertaken by Bishop Goldwell. His episcopate followed that of Walter Lyhart who had taken the responsibility for so many major works of reconstruction following the calamity of 1463. In Goldwell's time many of these tasks were completed, and to Goldwell's credit they were completed in a manner and style consistent with the inception of Lyhart's work of reconstruction. In particular the lierne vaulting that characterized the nave was continued in the presbytery. Goldwell had already shown his consistency in following Lyhart's initiation of the lierne style by his treatment of the vaulting of the Bauchun Chapel. The presbytery, however, presented an undertaking of far greater magnitude. The eastern part of the cathedral was the earliest built and most venerated. The area to be spanned by the vaulting covered the apsidal east end of the presbytery and the four bays reaching westward to the crossing beneath the tower. The total area is a little less than half that of the nave. A further consideration was that the vaulting had to be constructed 83 feet (25m) above ground level, 11 feet (3.3m) higher than in the nave. The difference arose because, whereas in the nave the vaulting sprang from the Norman capitals of the clerestory windows, in the presbytery it sprang from the midpoint of the fourteenth-century ogival arches between the windows, thus creating a steeper rise. The eye is drawn upwards dramatically, past the light-filled fourteenth-century windows to the stellar pattern of the fifteenth-century vaulting. The bosses, smaller and further away than those in the nave, emphasize this starry effect. The vaults of the nave and presbytery, John Harvey maintains, 'approaching the fan-vaulting in feeling, are ... among the finest in the country.'

The ethereal impact of the presbytery vaulting is brought about by a combination of the following: the height; the steeply rising ribs; the starry pattern; the light shining upwards from the tall clerestory windows; the smallness of the bosses compared with those of the nave; and their uniformity of subject matter.

There are one hundred and twenty-eight bosses in the presbytery. Care was taken to number them in photographs that were taken when they

The presbytery

overleaf

Two disciples prepare to have their feet washed (NJI5)

The Last Supper (NJI0 p.97) is the centre boss of this bay. Christ's washing the disciples feet is an essential part of the theology, drama, and iconography of this event. Christ washes Peter's feet, and this is shown in a nearby boss (NJI8). Here two disciples wait their turn. The one on the right has already taken off his left boot, which lies on the ground. His right leg is crossed over his left as he takes off the boot from his right foot. The disciple on the left holds up the instep of his shoe in his left hand. Perhaps this scene reflects the action of the fifteenth-century players who performed the parts of the disciples. Little attention was given to costume them as Jews of the first century AD. They were dressed for the most part in contemporary costume, and before they could have their feet washed they needed to take off their hose.

previous page
Christ before Pilate (NK10)

Christ is brought before Pilate to be inter-
rogated. Pilate is seated under a canopied
bench, representing the seat of justice. His
red hat is bordered with ermine; his gown
is speckled and has golden cuffs. His
hands are close together but held out towards Christ who stands before him with
his hands crossed on his breast. Behind
Christ stands a bearded figure holding a
mace or sceptre, perhaps Pilate's messen-
ger. The soldiers who have arrested Christ
stand behind him, one of them keeping
hold of him with his left arm. Immediately beneath the man with the sceptre
is the half figure of a tonsured priest, as
though Annas and Caiaphas have sent
a spy to report on the proceedings in
Pilate's court. On the extreme right, with
one hand clutching Pilate's throne, is
another eavesdropper.

were being cleaned in 1973. Ninety-four bosses are of gold wells, an in-
dulgent rebus on the bishop's name; twenty-nine are floral, mostly roses;
five, coming at the intersection of the transverse rib above the ogival arch
and the main ridge rib, are, from the east, (1) the Virgin Mary in Glory,
(2) God the Father supporting in front of him the crucified Christ, and
(3, 4, 5) bosses bearing Goldwell's crest or coats of arms. This group of
five bosses which are slightly larger than the others will be described first.

The Virgin in Glory (P83) stands in the centre of the carving. From a
red and gold crown her hair falls in straight lines, also of red and gold.
She wears a long red gown with golden diapers, over which is a golden
mantle with a blue lining. Her hands are held up, palms outward. Her
figure is rayed as though within a mandorla, an almond-shaped panel.
Beyond the pointed gold rays on either side are five red roses, and beyond
the roses blue clouds form the boss's periphery. The boss acts as the keystone to the ten adjoining ribs each of which is painted with elongated
foliate patterns as though to emphasize the eradiation stemming from
the Virgin in Glory.

The carving of God holding the crucified Christ in front of him shows
a similar ring of clouds on the periphery, and, within, set against the rays
of the sun, is the figure of God the Father. He is crowned, with long,
flowing, curly hair. With his two hands he holds up the arms of the cross
from underneath. His forked beard is just above Christ's head. Christ,
wearing the crown of thorns, dressed in a loin-cloth, hangs on the cross.
He too is bearded. His eyes appear closed. The wound in his side is bleeding. His body bears the marks of his scourging. No figure of the Holy
Ghost in the form of a dove is included. Painted on the eight adjoining
ribs and also on the roof of the vault are varieties of leaves and flowers
coloured red and green, forming an evocative background to a beautifully
carved boss. This technique of foliage painting, used so widely in the
presbytery vaulting but so little elsewhere, enhances the stellar effect.

Goldwell's shield of the see of Norwich, *azure with three mitres gold* (P47)
is supported by an angel on either side. Each wears long feathered garments with decorated tippets which at their lower edge are squarely

dagged. Leaves and flowers are painted on the adjoining vaulting.

What is questionably a cardinal's hat rests above the boss that displays Goldwell's coat of arms (P29). The so-called cardinal's hat has been taken as a reference to Goldwell's consecration in Rome by the President of the Pope's Chancery in 1472. Another attribution is to Thomas Bourchier, Archbishop of Canterbury, 1454-86. He was raised to the cardinalate in 1467 and the red hat was sent to him in 1473. His appointment as Cardinal was an honour reflected throughout the country. It is probably a carving of Bourchier wearing his cardinal's hat that appears on the corbel at the base of the north-west arch of the great west window. However, it might be wise to view with some caution the identification of this presbytery carving with that of a cardinal's hat, as it neither carries the usual form nor does it bear any cords or tassels. In the presbytery boss Goldwell's coat of arms is painted on the shield beneath the hat. The shield is supported on either side by an angel in feathered dress and ermine tippet.

Goldwell's armorial crest seen above his effigy on the south side of the presbytery is repeated in one of the centre bosses in the vaulting (P11). It shows an image of a helm surmounted by a well from which columbines spring. The effect is of cascading water. The bricks of the well are clearly marked. Leaves sprout from the top of the well. Acanthus leaves surround the helm. At the base of an angled shield is a lion rampant. The lion's tail curls along its back extending to above its head.

The twenty-nine bosses with a floral pattern are found on the periphery of the main design: bosses P1-6 are over the western arch; the others appear in groups of three as keystones for the ribs springing from the mid-point of the large fourteenth-century windows. The predominant form is the Tudor rose. Leaves are sometimes carved on the boss but also painted on to the surrounding vaulting.

The ninety-four wells appear in a great variety of forms, but most of them are surrounded by painted foliage on the vaulting. The foliage most frequently depicted is that of clover and hellebore. The wells themselves are sometimes surrounded by carvings of large leaves (P12) or with leaves

overleaf
Malchus' ear (NK17)

'Simon Peter therefore having a sword drew it, and struck the high priest's servant, and cut off his right ear.'

John 18. 10.

Malchus' ear on Peter's sword becomes one of the signs of Christ's Passion. The quire of Winchester Cathedral has an array of wooden roof bosses devoted to the symbols of Christ's Passion, one of them being the sword with the ear affixed. In this carving Peter's sword has severed the ear which sticks to the middle of the blade. Malchus half kneels in front of Christ who will heal him. Between Peter and Malchus is a large lantern, a property regularly associated with Malchus who leads the search at night to arrest Christ. The high priest's men come with 'cressets, and lanterns, and torches'.

previous page
The Buffeting of Christ (NK15)

'And the men that held Jesus mocked him, and beat him. And they blindfolded him, and asked him, saying, Prophesy, who is he that struck thee?'

Luke 22. 63, 64.

Christ is blindfolded, seated on a bench. He is held in position by the two torturers behind him. The one on the left has a hand on his shoulder and a hand on his head. The one on the right also has a hand on his shoulder, but with his right fist is about to punch Christ on the head. He sticks out his tongue in mockery. This is a small boss. It appears that the torturers are taking it in turn to hit Christ on the head. In the Wakefield mystery cycle there is a play of *The Buffetting of Christ* where such a scene is enacted. In that part of Yorkshire children still play a game called 'hot cockles' based on this incident from the Bible.

overleaf
Dicing for Christ's garment (NL7)

'Let us not rend it, but cast lots for it, whose it shall be.'

John 19. 24.

Two men are playing dice for Christ's garment, the seamless robe. Their dice are as large as their heads. They are seated on a green sward on which flowers are painted. Spread between them is Christ's garment, gold with a white lining; the neck and sleeves are under the players' feet. The

man on the left has his right hand still on the dice. He has thrown a five, a four and a one. It would seem a winning combination because the figure on the right points to the four with his left hand and strikes his opponent on the head with his right hand.

In the great east window of St Peter Mancroft, Norwich, a stained glass representation of this scene shows the two dice players with their daggers drawn. The medieval plays on this subject, Chaucer's *Tales*, and the experience of the centuries testify that dicing often ends in physical violence.

A set of dice also appears in a wooden roof boss in the quire of Winchester Cathedral as a symbol of Christ's Passion.

sprouting from the top (P22, 23, 24, 36, 37, 38). The general appearance of the bosses is of foreshortened pillar-boxes or squat capstans. They stand alone or are supported by angels who hold the wells in front of them in their arms. Sometimes the angel's tippet overlaps the top of the well (P87, 89) and sometimes the angel sports spotted sleeves (P26, 28, 30, 61, 75). At times the angel holds a shield on which the well is painted not carved (P7, 8, 9, 13, 14, 15, 19, 20, 21). The hole in the presbytery main ridge, although smaller than the hole in the nave ridge, probably served the same purpose, that of the lowering of the sacrament or a censing angel on special occasions. In the presbytery the hole appears in the middle of a boss (P56) which has a well sculptured around it. The hole thus seems to be the top of the well from which emerge draped long leaves. The vaulted background is painted with leaves and globular fruit.

The presbytery bosses, with their proliferation of gold wells and Goldwell's other armorial insignia, trumpet out the bishop's ostentation and self-aggrandizement. In the vaulting of the area of the cathedral held most holy the bishop has blazoned his own importance. Yet the viewer, putting aside the bishop's self-absorption, will readily be persuaded that the artistic achievement of the presbytery vaulting is of the highest order, and the instantaneous aesthetic satisfaction of gazing upwards is breathtaking and deeply memorable.

The Transepts

Numbering system for the transept roof bosses

There are seventy-five narrative roof bosses in each of the transepts. In each transept there are twenty-five bosses in each of the central, east, and west sections. NT stands for north transept; ST for south transept. Roof bosses along the central ridge are identified by the letter C after NT or ST. Bosses to the east or west of the central ridge are identified by the letter E or W after NT or ST.
The narrative begins at the north end of the north transept with NTC1, NTE1, NTW1, and progresses to the south end of the north transept where the last three bosses are numbered NTC25, NTE25, NTW25. The narrative in the south transept begins over its northern arch with STC1, STE1, STW1, and concludes over its southern arch with STC25, STE25, and STW25.

IN 1509 following a fire in the transepts a new stone vaulting was erected during the episcopate of Richard Nykke (1501-36). The bishop was not an attractive personality, and few record anything to his credit. In 1536 he died in prison, penniless, blind, and out of favour with his king. But he merits praise, at least, for re-building the roof of the transepts in stone. When incendiary bombs struck the roof of the transepts in 1942 it was Bishop Nykke's stone vaulting which prevented a major conflagration.

At the time of the 1509 fire a stellar pattern of lierne stone vaulting covered the nave, the presbytery, and the Bauchun Chapel. For Nykke to have replaced the transepts' earlier wooden roofs with Tudor wooden ceilings would not only have been cheaper and quicker, but also more fashionable. In any case, at this time, he was already probably contemplating the Tudor alterations to the south aisle of the nave, part of which became a chantry chapel at which mass-priests were to pray for his soul. Instead he decided to rebuild both the south and north transepts in the style that his predecessors, Lyhart and Goldwell, had adopted when faced with roofing repairs. And so it is that the stellar-patterned lierne stone vaulting in both transepts completes a homogeneous roofing scheme, at the highest level, throughout the cathedral.

Whereas Lyhart's nave roof with its fourteen bays contained a highly systemised array of storied bosses, Goldwell's magnificent presbytery roof with its five bays abandoned any system of storied bosses. Goldwell's 'system' was the proliferation of gold wells. Nykke, in the transepts, re-introduced storied bosses.

There are four bays in each of the transepts. In the middle of each of

previous page
Mixing the vinegar and gall (NL8)

A cylindrical vessel with an indented panel on its side and a ringed handle stands within the groin of the boss. Two men lean over the vessel. The one on the right wears a gown tied at the waist with a red belt. He might be emptying gall from the pouch-like container in his hands into the receptacle. Close by is a bearded figure holding the head of a sponge in his left hand. He wears a close-fitting red cap that partly covers his shoulders like a balaclava helmet. The sponge dipped in vinegar and gall will be lifted to Christ's mouth as he approaches death on the cross as seen in the boss of the crucifixion (NL10 p.112).

overleaf
The Crucifixion (NL10)

The cross is aligned along the main ridge of the vaulting. Apart from Christ, the figures carved around the cross are mostly positioned in the groins of the ribs. Many of their faces are tilted upwards towards the cross. Christ is a passive figure. Around him is seen the intense activity of the soldiers, mocking and gesturing. Ten figures are gathered round the cross. Christ hangs from the cross by the two nails which pierce his palms. One nail penetrates both feet. Both shins and feet appear to be replacements. The crown of plaited thorns is set upon his golden hair which hangs down on either side over his armpits. His beard is forked. The head and shoulders of two soldiers are seen above the cross. The gold tips of their halberds glint against a dark background. Another two helmeted soldiers are seen on either side behind the foot of the cross.

the bays is a transverse rib which spans from the centre point of the arch of the east clerestory gallery to the centre point of the arch of the west clerestory gallery. At the lower levels of these transverse arches are three bosses on either side which are not associated with the storied system. These bosses which number forty-eight in all mostly depict Bishop Nykke's arms: *azure with three mitres gold* (the arms of the see); and *gold with a chevron between three leopards' heads gules* (the arms of the bishop).

In addition to these forty-eight bosses there are a further seventy-five bosses in each of the transepts, set out in a similar pattern to that obtaining in the nave: eighteen bosses in each bay ($4 \times 18 = 72$) and three additional bosses in the southernmost arches of each transept. The system of numbering the bosses is described in the note on the coding of the transepts, see page 107. The 'story-telling' begins at the north end of the north transept and continues to the south end of the south transept. The subject of the transepts deals with the birth and early life of both John the Baptist and Christ.

C. J. P. Cave, whose book *Roof Bosses in Medieval Churches*, has remained for many years the standard work on the subject, has also written a number of separate booklets on roof bosses found in particular cathedrals: Winchester, Chester, Exeter, for example. His lecture on *The Roof Bosses in the Transepts of Norwich Cathedral* was delivered in 1932 and published in Oxford in 1933. Cave acknowledges his debt to Dr W. T. Bensly who had given an account of these bosses at the annual meeting of the Norfolk and Norwich Archaeological Society in 1893. A few months earlier, while work was being undertaken on the transepts, part of which had involved the removal of the brown wash on the walls and the roof, Bensly had taken the opportunity of having the bosses photographed. He also made full notes describing the bosses and recording the colours revealed. His own account of the colours of the transept bosses, together with Goulburn's records of the colours of the nave bosses twenty years earlier, are valuable historical data, because there would have been no attempt whatsoever to repaint the bosses from the time of the Reformation to the time that the wash was removed. The brown wash had by great good fortune preserved the pristine colouring. As the wash was being removed one can imagine the excitement and delight of the recorders. The medieval colours had been left intact in the nave and transept bosses whereas the cloister bosses had mostly lost their medieval colouring through the weathering of the centuries.

Both Cave for the transept bosses and Goulburn for the nave bosses differ at times with Bensly's ascription of subject. But Cave makes full use of Bensly's notes and photographs. It is clear that Cave's description of the bosses is mainly from his looking at the photographs in front of him. For this method to be satisfactory it is essential to have at least three or four photographs of the same boss shot from different angles. This he did not have, and although he reveals so much to us that cannot be seen with the naked eye nor with any steadiness through binoculars, there are a number of instances where the details of the full carving were hidden from him. However, our indebtedness to Cave is considerable for, without his work on the transepts, interest in these carvings might have remained at a low ebb because of M. R. James's severe strictures about their design and execution.

James believed that Bishop Nykke was hard pressed to think of a satisfactory theme for the bosses: 'He must have decided to supplement the New Testament portion of Lyhart's work by filling up gaps in the life of the Virgin and of Christ. But he was not fortunate in his designer, or in his clerk of works. The former had very little invention, and did not care how often he repeated his subject, whilst the latter took no pains whatever to get the bosses put up in a rational order. Nor does the execution of the carving reflect credit on any one. The whole work, in fact, gives the impression of haste and carelessness.'

Cave accepts the charge of repetition: the Flight occurs eight times; the angel appearing to St Joseph nine times; and the Nativity three times. But he maintains, nevertheless, that there are some 'very charming little carvings'. His close study of the bosses led him to a more appreciative view than James's. But both James and Cave are dismissive of what they consider repetitive work, without their detecting in a sequence of carvings

To the right of the cross a helmeted soldier raises a sponge set on the end of a red pole towards Christ. He has a chin-guard and wears over his shoulders a red, dagged tippet, beneath which shows his armour. Above him is another soldier, bearded, helmeted, richly arrayed. In his left hand he holds a halberd and with his right hand seems to be drawing from its scabbard a short sword. On the left of the cross is a soldier who peers out from under Christ's right arm. On the extreme left is another soldier in full armour, with helmet, breastplate and articulated skirt-armour. He carries a broad-bladed spear in his right hand. Slightly below him is the blind knight, Longinus, who thrusts up a spear, now broken, into Christ's right side. The apocryphal story of Longinus, included in the *N-Town Play*, is of a knight who has been blind for thirty years, who is confronted by the soldiers as he passes by the scene of the crucifixion. He has a spear thrust into his hands and is made to strike it upwards into the side of Christ. The blood flows from the wound on to Longinus' hand. As he wipes his eyes with his hand he regains his sight and realizes the enormity of his deed. This carving shows Longinus, having pierced Christ's side, putting his bloodstained hand to his eyes. Above the upright of the cross a wooden pole is split at the top to carry the scroll on which is written INRI (Jesus of Nazarus, the King of the Jews).

In the 1870s, when scaffolding was erected in the nave, Dean Goulburn was able to note the dimensions of the cross: the total length of the upright is 22 inches (55cm) of which 1¾ inches (4.4cm) appear above the transverse beam. The transverse beam measures 17 inches (42.5cm); the width of the upright is just over 2 inches (5cm).

previous page
The unjust alewife (NN7)

A devil with cloven hoofs pushes a wheelbarrow in which there sits a naked, damned soul. The devil, also naked, has ginger hair, a scarred face, and a large nose. His mouth is wide open as he leers at his victim gleefully. The damned soul has short black hair, cut in a pudding-basin style. His arms and hands cover his face, signalling his terror of what is to come. On the devil's back, sitting astride his shoulders, is a woman with long black hair that streams down her shoulders and back. She too is naked. With her left hand she clutches the devil's hair to steady herself, and with her right hand she holds aloft defiantly a large tankard. In contrast to the devil's victim in the wheelbarrow her expression is exuberant. She represents the alewife who gives false measure. She is to be found regularly among the damned, as in the chancel painting of the Last Judgement in St. Thomas's Church, Salisbury.

on the same theme incremental differences, such as one might notice in a sequence of drawings that comprises an animated cartoon. Furthermore, James's charge that the clerk of works took no pains at all to get the bosses put up in a rational order is scarcely tenable. The rational order of the main ridge bosses in the south walk of the cloisters is apparent. The sequence follows in linear form the page-by-page illustrations from an illuminated manuscript of the Revelation of St John the Divine. But no such 'rational order' exists in the arrangement of the bosses in the nave where, bay by bay, the theme of the carving is set by the main centre boss, and that theme is taken up in a radial way by the satellite bosses that comprise the lierne vaulting stellar pattern. The transept pattern follows that of the nave not that of the south walk of the cloisters. There is a perceptible and steady progression in the thematic treatment. For instance the four bays in the north transept might be seen to progress as follows:

from the north

BAY 1   The Birth of John the Baptist
          The preparation for the Annunciation
          The Annunciation

BAY 2   The Nativity
          The Shepherds follow the star

BAY 3   The Adoration of the Shepherds
          The Adoration of the Magi

BAY 4   The Flight into Egypt
          The Massacre of the Innocents
          The Death of Herod

The south transept also, despite a few anomalies, has the bosses arranged, bay by bay, showing a clear chronological progression.

from the north

BAY 1   The early life of Christ
        Christ in the Temple

BAY 2   The Temptations
        Calling the Disciples

BAY 3   The First Miracle
        John the Baptist and Herod

BAY 4   Christ's ministry of healing

Among the anomalies in the south transept are the repetition of scenes already depicted in the north transept bosses such as the Flight into Egypt (STE1 and STW3), the Presentation in the Temple (STC1, STE7, and STC7), and the Circumcision of Jesus (STW7). Also the scenes of Christ's baptism by John appear both in the first and third bays (STC5 p.128 and STC13), between which are carvings of the temptations of Christ and Christ calling together his disciples.

The choice of subjects for the transept bosses remains something of an enigma. James's conclusion that Bishop Nykke's intention was to 'supplement the New Testament portion of Lyhart's work, by filling up gaps in the life of the Virgin and of Christ' fails to take account of the considerable emphasis in the transept carvings given to John the Baptist. It is true, however, that one of the strangest omissions among the nave carvings is the representation of the adoration of the shepherds and the Magi. One boss (NH14 p.85) shows two shepherds on their way to the manger, and two bosses depict the Magi journeying with their gifts: two kings on one (NH12), and one on the other (NH11). The fundamental difference in thematic treatment, however, between the carving of the nave bosses and those of the transepts is that, whereas the nave takes an Old or New Testament subject and deals with it in broad outline, the transepts take a more limited subject and deal with it in stage-by-stage detail. For instance, in the nave the eighth bay, Bay H, deals with the Nativity. There

overleaf

Good souls being led into heaven (NN16)

'And he shall send forth his angels with a great sound of a trumpet, and they shall gather together the elect from the four winds, from one end of heaven to the other.'

Matthew 24. 31.

The centre boss of the westernmost bay in the nave is of Christ sitting in judgement (NN10 p.117) with angels blowing the last trump on either side of him. The surrounding bosses show the dead rising from their graves, devils carrying off the doomed to hell, and there are two bosses in which the angels are leading the elect to heaven. Here an angel has his left hand raised in benediction and with his right hand he holds the wrist of a saved soul whom he is leading to heaven. Behind walks another saved soul whose hands are raised in wonder and thankfulness.

previous page
The Last Judgement (NN10)

Christ is enthroned upon a rainbow. The
sun's rays eradiate behind him and the
crescent moon is at his feet. Christ wears
a plaited crown of thorns beneath which
falls his golden hair. His beard too is
golden. Both his hands are held up, palms
outwards, showing the stigmata. His mantle rests on his shoulders but leaves his
torso bare, revealing the wound in his side.
On either side, emerging from clouds, is
an angel blowing a trumpet. Each angel
has curly golden hair over which is a skull-
cap and a golden circlet carrying a cross in
front. In the earth beneath, marked by
branches and roots, two figures emerge
from their tombs. On the right a naked
portly figure has his right arm and leg out
of his coffin. His head is twisted round to
look at Christ with some apprehension.
On the head is the triple tiara of a pope.
Behind him another figure emerges. He is
naked apart from his tall, jewelled crown.
His hands are held together in prayer.
The inference might be that the king on
the right of the Judgement Seat will be
welcomed into heaven; the pope on the
left will be doomed to hell.
Dean Goulburn noted in the 1870s that
the head and hands of the Christ figure
and the hands and arms of the king had
been lost but replaced in the restoration
work of that decade.

are eighteen carvings that cover the story from the Annunciation to the
Massacre of the Innocents. But the treatment is not detailed in an incremental way as it is in the treatment of the Annunciation in the first bay
of the north transept. God instructs Gabriel to visit Mary (NTC4 and
NTE5); Gabriel leaves heaven's gates (NTW5) and approaches a doorway
above which is a four-pointed star. The Annunciation scene (NTW3) shows
Mary at a reading desk on which is an open book. The winged angel of
the Annunciation stands beneath an arch on the left. A pot of lilies stands
between them. This might be viewed almost as a standard model for an
Annunciation scene, but the follow-up scene is of Mary, still reading,
framed in an archway, while to the right the angel speaks to Joseph
assuring him of Mary's purity, and admonishing him for his suspicions.
There are other bosses also associated with the Annunciation (NTW6,
NTC7, NTW7, NTE8) which fill in many more details of the story.

Within this context of charting small shifts in movement according to
the progress of the story, the criticism of poverty of invention, even for
the eight carvings associated with the Flight into Egypt, is scarcely
justified. With regard to the Flight the carver is intent to show various
phases of the journey out of Bethlehem (NTE25) and through the gateway
into Egypt (NTW25) and meeting Pharaoh (NTC20). The last bosses in the
north transept are on the theme of Flight. It is likely that the first bosses
in the south transept on this theme of Joseph leading Mary who is
mounted signal the return from Egypt. Mary is invariably shown riding
side-saddle, holding her swaddled child in her arms. It is reported that
the first time the people of Norwich saw anyone riding side-saddle was
in 1383, when King Richard II and his Queen, Anne of Bohemia, visited
the city. Fine ladies might thereafter be seen riding side-saddle, but not
the peasants. The carving in the west walk of the cloister (CWA6) shows
the peasant woman astride a horse as she carries over her shoulders a sack
of corn to the windmill to be ground.

The transept carvings contain a range of recognizable attributes that
help identify the characters. Peter holds a key (STE22, STW22, STC21, STW11,
STC10), Andrew a saltire cross (STW11, STC10, STE9, STW9), and James wears

his pilgrim's hat embossed with a shell (STC8). Herodias is always crowned and lifts her dress off the ground with one hand. A lady-in-waiting often stands behind her holding up her train (STC15, STE14, STC18, STW17). Joseph usually carries a red walking stick which has a right-angled handle. Herod the Great is marked by his crossed legs which make him seem contorted, or by the devil that with red eyes and red lips leers from out of the top of Herod's crown (NTE23, NTW23, NTE21, NTE15). In the south transept John the Baptist wears a sleeveless gown, and Christ carries an orb in his left hand. As these two figures appear so frequently such a differentiation is immediately helpful. Salome is recognized by her acrobatic dancing before Herod at his birthday feast. As she dances with a sword in her left hand she bends over backwards beneath the level of the table (STC19). She also appears again in this carving sitting on Herod's right at the table. The north walk boss in the cloisters (CNG5) also features the double appearance of Salome, and in that boss her dancing posture is very similar to that seen here.

While it cannot be claimed that the quality of the carving is as zestful and energetic as that of the nave or the cloisters, there is, nevertheless, a great deal to commend it. A number of hands were responsible for the work. It must be admitted that the execution of some of the carving is stiff, formalized, and cramped. This is particularly true of the many bosses that portray feasts (STC14, STC16, STW16). Yet, as Cave remarked, there is much that is full of charm. The Annunciation group in its use of arches, angles, and double scenes, conveys movement, contrast, and grace. Similarly, the bosses depicting the three kings in their various journeyings are attractive in the detail of differentiation and in the delicacy with which the three are shown on the smallest of the bosses, mounted and bearing their gifts, and above all in their presentation scenes, the approach to the Holy Family (NTC16) and the offering of their gifts (NTW16).

In the south transept a number of scenes with boats are carved by a sculptor with a sharp sense of composition and, it would seem, with an intimate knowledge of the vessels and their tackle (STC8 p.129, STC10 p.133, STW11, STC20, STW20). Perhaps these carvers at the beginning of the

overleaf

The three shepherds come to Bethlehem (NTC18)

The three shepherds approach the gates of a walled city. They have come to a closed four-panelled door with two metal hinges. Above the arched doorway is a circular window set in a stepped gable. To the right is the wall of the town with a looped window, and adjoining is a turret with a quatrefoil opening. Within the town is the roof of a gabled house with a circular window beneath the gable, under which is an oblong window set with two mullions. To the left of the doorway and above the first shepherd's head has been carved a stiff-leaved tree.

The three shepherds are clearly on the move. The first shepherd has his left foot on the threshold of the doorway. His head is turned outwards. He is dressed in a pleated bonnet with a turned-up brim. The front of his knee-length tunic is also pleated. He wears black shoes over wine-coloured hose. He is playing the bagpipes and squeezing the air-bag under his right arm. His hands are holding the two chanters or melody-pipes, and the fingers of his left hand are on the stops. Behind him the second shepherd points with his left hand to the door. He wears a round hat with turned-up brim. Over his right shoulder he carries a crook. He wears a tippet and a belt from which hangs a pouch. On his feet are laced ankle-boots. The third shepherd has a cowl-like hat pulled well down over his forehead. His chin also is protected. He carries a crook in his right hand, and in his left hand he holds what might be a casket or, as in a neighbouring boss (NTC14), a basket with a handle on top. He wears boots which cover his knees.

previous page
The death of Herod (NTW22)

Herod lies in bed dying. His eyes are open. He wears his crown which is decorated with large round holes as though they once held precious jewels. His black hair falls to his shoulders and he has a black beard. His head rests on a pillow with a patterned edge. A white sheet is turned down over a golden coverlet, which is carved in ridges. Herod appears naked although only his chest and right arm are showing above the coverlet. Three mourners in various postures of grief lean over the bed on the far side. Each wears a large hat with upturned brim, but in each case the style is distinct. The one on the left has his left hand on the sheet and wipes his eye with his right hand in which he might be holding a rolled-up handkerchief. The mourner in the middle with lips turned down and clasping both hands together in front of him looks extremely sour. The man on the right leans on the bed with his left elbow. He has a short beard. His eyes are nearly closed as though he has fallen asleep.

sixteenth century when manuscripts were being replaced by printed books, felt less reliant on either source and were using their own inventiveness more. This might be borne out by the very graphic carving of John the Baptist preaching from a pulpit (STC12 p.124). The boss in its clarity and vitality, knitting the auditors to the preacher, seems to be making a statement about the contemporary stress on preaching, which was certainly a plank in the reformists' platform. The same hand probably carved Jesus with the Doctors in the temple (STC2), another highly skilled piece of work. It contrasts the young boy, simply dressed, his hair short-cropped, but seated in a raised high-backed chair, with the doctors, in their patterned gowns and furred tippets, gathered close about him. Each doctor, apart from one, appears to be disputing some religious text drawn from the open book which he holds. Only one looks directly at Christ, and in his right hand is a closed book.

The roof bosses of the transepts were the last to be carved in Norwich Cathedral. The bishop who had instructed the work to be undertaken was shortly to be imprisoned and disgraced; and thirty years after the fire in the south transept the Priory itself was dissolved. The day of the Cathedral craftsmen seemed past, especially as they viewed the destruction of their work in the shrines dedicated to the saints, and of those images on reredoses, retables, in niches, and in chantry chapels. But desecrating the roof bosses seventy or eighty feet up was a more daunting task. It was that inaccessibility and the periodic application of a coat of white or brown wash that helped to preserve for us an inestimable treasure.

overleaf **John the Baptist preaching** (STC12)

John the Baptist is in a sleeveless hair-shirt, albeit painted gold. He is apparently preaching to the Pharisees and Sadducees (Matthew 3. 7) the lower four of whom are looking for the authority of his words in their sacred texts.
John, who has long golden hair and a golden beard, has his left hand placed on top of a hexagonal pulpit and his right hand on his breast. The forefinger of this hand is pointed as though 'the one who is to come'. Six figures act as auditors, three either side of the pulpit. On the right a bearded face appears level with John's, clad in a large red hat with wide brim turned up and flattened in

Drama and the Roof Bosses

THE apsidal chapel on the south of the ambulatory was dedicated to St Luke in 1422. Among his many attributes St Luke was the patron saint of painters and other craftsmen. In Norwich the Guild of St Luke was a socio-religious organization comprising a range of craftsmen including painters, glaziers, pewterers, braziers, bell-founders, plumbers, all crafts closely associated with the rebuilding, repair and decoration of the cathedral, the priory, and the other extensive property within the Close. Throughout most of the fifteenth century and for the first quarter of the sixteenth this guild was responsible for much of the seasonal entertainment in Norwich. In 1527 the guild complained to the mayor and the city assembly that they felt they could no longer undertake these responsibilities because of the expense, the unfair burden on their members, and because at festive times when Norwich was full of visitors it was an occasion for other crafts to thrive while the guild of St Luke was at full stretch providing and paying for the entertainment. The guild's petition mentions the range of entertainment that it had been providing on Whit Monday and Tuesday 'of long time past': various 'disguisings', pageants, processions, representations of the lives and martyrdoms of the saints, and 'pictures of other persons and beasts'. We may gather from this that the range of entertainment offered was both serious and light. The city assembly responded to their petition by relieving the guild of its onerous responsibilities and requiring the other guilds to bear their part. In consequence a document that can be dated about 1530 provides us with a list of sixty-four guilds who are to present pageants on a range of subjects usually associated with the Corpus Christi procession

front. Beneath him is a man with a golden, rolled-brim hat with a dark pleated cloth hanging down either side. He wears an ermine tippet and a golden gown. In his hands he holds a book, closed with a clasp. His left hand rests on top of the book. He is seated on the rib of the boss. At the lowest level on his right side is a third man in a squatting position. He has a small pointed, black beard, a close-fitting headdress with a black rounded crown on which is a golden band. From this band on either side fall red triangular lappets with golden tassels. He wears a tippet with large smudgy brown spots, and he holds an open book in front of him to which he points with his right hand. On the left at the lowest level is a younger man in a close-fitting hat with a bobble on top. He wears a red pleated gown patterned with golden diapers. His left hand is held to his forehead. His right hand is placed before him on an open book. In the middle position on the left is a golden-bearded man with a red tippet with a patterned edge. His dome-like hat, divided by a central band, is like a bishop's mitre. He has all the dignity and appearance of a high priest. He also holds in his hands an open book. Top left is another bearded head with a hat similar to that top right.

The design of the pulpit is similar to that to be seen in the east window of the chancel of St Peter Mancroft, Norwich, which depicts St Peter preaching to the people.

previous page
The Holy Innocents (NTC22)

This boss in the north transept is one of a cluster dealing with the massacre of the innocent children and the death of Herod. Its iconography is rare within a Nativity sequence. It shows the souls of the massacred children being received into heaven. Three naked children stand together with their hands clasped in prayer. Each has long golden hair. They are escorted by four angels standing at their level. The inwardly curved wings of the outer angels add to the feeling of protectiveness. Above them are three more angels of which the one in the centre wears a full ermine tippet and plays a four-stringed lute with a peg-box bent back at an angle from the neck.

The disappearance of the two princes in the Tower of London in 1483 led to the belief that they had been murdered by Richard III who within his life-time was likened to Herod. A carving of the Holy Innocents might well have had political resonances within the first few decades of the Tudor dynasty.

and play. For instance *Paradise* (Adam and Eve) is given to the Grocers and Chandlers; *Noah's Ship* is the responsibility of the Bakers, Brewers, Innkeepers, Cooks, Millers, Vintners, and Coopers. Also listed is *The Conflict of David and Goliath* to be undertaken by the Smiths' Guild. None of the extant English mystery cycles includes such a play. The seventh bay of the nave vaulting contains the story of David and Goliath: the subject is also treated in the cloister carvings.

Of the Norwich Guilds' participation in the Corpus Christi plays only one significant record has come down to us. It is that of the Norwich Grocers. Two versions are derived from eighteenth-century copies but neither the sixteenth-century originals nor the eighteenth-century copies have survived. The two survivors are nineteenth-century redactions. Evidence from the Grocers' accounts indicates that performances were given in 1534 and on a number of occasions annually up to and including 1565. There is no record of a performance after 1565. No performances were given in 1539 and 1540, the years immediately following the dissolution of the monasteries.

The Grocers' accounts between 1534 and 1565 give particulars relating to both processions and performances. Most significantly they give details of a very substantial four-wheeled cart with a large superstructure made of wainscotting and gaily painted. It had a square roof on top of which is a gilded griffin, the Grocers' emblem, with a flag flying above. Their play of *Paradise* tells of the Serpent tempting Adam and Eve, and their banishment from the garden of Eden. Properties and costumes are detailed. On the Tree of Knowledge hang all sorts of fruit: oranges, figs, almonds, dates, raisins, prunes, and apples. In 1565 the actor playing the serpent needs a coat, hose, and a painted tail, together with a white wig. Adam and Eve also have wigs. God the Father has both a mask and a wig. In 1547 a wig and crown are made for the Angel, who drives Adam and Eve out of Paradise; and in 1565 this Angel is provided with a coat and 'over-hose' of ape's skin. The roof boss depicting the temptation of Adam and Eve (NA11, front cover) has the tree set in a portable stand. The action also represents the passing of the apple from the Serpent to Eve to Adam:

the three characters have their hands on five apples to chart the movement of one apple rather than five. The Serpent's tail, wound round the tree, is painted gold. At waist level Satan wears a golden garment that seems to be attached to the tail, but if staged as the boss appears, the rest of Satan's body might be concealed behind the tree. The upper part of the body is that of a female, and the wig which is fair, if not white, is curled and crowned with a thin fillet.

The nave bosses were carved sixty years or so before the first of the available Grocers' accounts were written, when the play of *Paradise* was not the responsibility of the Grocers but of St Luke's Guild. Furthermore the plays were constantly being rewritten in the light of religious, political, and social changes. The two versions of *Paradise*, 1534 and 1565, show marked differences: the one written at the beginning of the Reformation but while Norwich Priory was still in being, and the other seven years into Elizabeth's strongly Protestant reign, after the dissolution of the Priory, and on the threshold of the plays' final suppression. That *David and Goliath* is listed as a pageant in *c.*1530 probably indicates that it was a pageant in the Corpus Christi processions of the fifteenth century. Certainly the vigorous treatment of this story in the roof bosses would support this. That the Smiths' guild was in charge in the later phases of this play's presentation might have reflected their involvement from much earlier times in helping to make Goliath's spectacular armour and weaponry.

The Grocers' accounts of 1534 indicate payment (12d=5 pence) to actors:

Item to Jeffrey Tybnam playing the Father	16d
Item to Mr Leman's servant playing Adam	6d
Item to Francis Fygot playing Eve	4d
Item to Thomas Wolf playing the Angel	4d
Item to Edmund Thurston playing the Serpent	4d
Item to John Bakyn playing at the organ	6d

overleaf

The Baptism of Christ (STC5)

Christ stands naked in the water which reaches to his knees. His hands are held together in prayer. John the Baptist, in a sleeveless gown tied at the waist, stands on dry land. With his right hand he holds over Christ's head an inverted pitcher from which flows a stream of blue water. Behind John on the right is a bare-headed tall figure. On the left are two others on dry land. The foremost is sitting down removing his hose in anticipation of entering the water and being baptised. The carving is small, homely, and unambitious compared with the nave boss on the same theme (NII0). In both the convention is maintained of John staying on dry ground while Christ stands in the water, and of a large pitcher of water, held in John's right hand, being inverted over Christ's head.

previous page
Christ calling his disciples (STC8)

Christ stands on the shore with two disciples, James and John. On the left Peter sits in a boat. With his right hand he holds a net in the water, and with his left hand he clutches the mast above which is a furled sail. Standing on dry land is John, beardless, and without a hat. He wears a long gown and in his hand he holds a chalice from which emerges a serpent. Above him is the bearded figure of James wearing his pilgrim's hat embossed with a scallop shell. The chalice and the shell are the attributes peculiar, respectively, to John and James. On the right is a boyish Jesus holding in his hands an orb, perhaps preaching to the people on shore.

Item for a horse	12d
Item for a ½ barrel of beer	10d
Item for bread, beef, veal, mutton, and other victuals, with the dressing	4s.6d

This extract from the accounts reveals that food and drink for the actors' rehearsals and performance are substantial perquisites. Payment for the horse drawing the pageant is more than that given to most of the actors. Tybnam is paid 16d for playing God. It is not the longest part, but level of payment probably matches seniority within the guild. Francis Fygot, a man, played the part of Eve. Women's parts were played by men. The musician on the portable organ was rewarded rather more than most of the actors. The actor playing the part of Adam is not named. Mr Leman, his master, perhaps not even a member of the guild, had in his service a good actor who at such times was in demand. Sir John Paston, a notable Norfolk landowner, had a game-keeper who was much in demand for playing the parts of St George and Robin Hood. In a letter, dated 16 April 1473, Paston complains bitterly of his man leaving his service. The servant's acting prowess had redounded to his master's credit.

It is from the Paston letters that we have the clearest indication that the Corpus Christi Plays were performed in Norwich. John Whetley writing to his master, John Paston II, on 20 May 1478, describes the Duke of Suffolk breaking into Hellesdon, one of the Paston manor houses, on the outskirts of Norwich. The Duke challenges Paston's right to the manor. He damages the property, seizes the fish from the fish pond, behaves in an overbearing way to the servants remaining in the house. Whetley writes

'... there was never no man that played Herod in Corpus Christi play better and more agreeable to his pageant than he did. But ye shall understand that it was after noon, and the weather hot, and he so feeble for sickness that his legs would not bear him, but there was two men had great pain to keep him on his feet ...'

Whetley writes his letter from Norwich on Corpus Christi Eve. He was probably thinking of going to see the plays in Norwich the next day. The character of Herod as a tyrannical ranter and ruthless child-slayer was among the most memorable of the Corpus Christi dramatis personae. Carvings of Herod abound in the cathedral vaulting. In the eighth bay of the nave where the bosses focus on the events of the Nativity, between two images of the Massacre of the Innocents is one of Herod, whose legs seem to be folding and he is supported on either side by one of his soldiers, each with a drawn sword (NH18).

East Anglia is the region richest in extant texts of medieval drama. The drama comprises a great mystery cycle, the *N-Town Play*, morality plays among which are *The Castle of Perseverance*, *Mankind*, and *Wisdom*, and plays about saints such as St Paul and Mary Magdalene. A feature common to many of these plays is that they were probably performed in the round. Acting stations were on the periphery of a circle, with the audience seated in the spaces between the acting stations. Processional scenes, such as the journey of the Magi or the carrying of the cross to Calvary, took place within the circle. In such a setting, as an action was ending in one area another was beginning nearby. The narrative action portrayed in the nave and transept roof bosses echoes such a pattern. At times the plays portray scenes, often from an apocryphal source, which are not replicated in the drama of other regions. When such scenes are found carved into the cathedral's roof bosses we must assume the closest association between the drama and the sculpture, and even, possibly, between the actor and the craftsman. The killing of Cain by the blind archer, Lamech, is such an example. It is written into the *N-Town Play* but is found in no other English mystery cycle. The subject is found dramatically carved in the nave vaulting (NA18).

Also within the *N-Town Play* is the scene of Pilate together with Caiaphas and Annas, the high priests, sealing the tomb in which Christ has been buried. They take this measure hoping thereby to prevent the body being stolen or mysteriously spirited away. A boss in the north walk of the cloister (CNA5 p.25) shows Pilate and his courtiers one side of the

overleaf
Christ healing the sick (STC22)

The vault bosses in the last bay, the southernmost, of the south transept are mainly concerned with the early ministry of Christ: on board ship with his disciples (STC20, STW20, STC23); casting out devils (STW23); and healing the sick (STC21, STE22, STC22, STW22, STE23). In this boss Christ stands centrally, surrounded by ten figures who come to him to be healed. In this transept's carvings Christ is consistently portrayed with boyish features. In his left hand he holds an orb, a symbol of his divine power; his right hand is held up in blessing. The bearded figure on Christ's left holds up his son's leg towards Christ for it to be healed. Immediately in front of Christ are two cripples. The one on the left, with his back turned to the viewer, is dressed in a short, red diapered tunic. The stump of his right leg is bandaged, and the knee rests in the cupped support of a wooden leg. The cripple on his right leans forward gripping a crutch in either hand.

previous page

The calling of Simon and Andrew (STC10)

'And walking by the sea of Galilee, he saw two brethren, Simon who is called Peter, and Andrew his brother, casting a net into the sea; for they were fishers. And he saith unto them, Come ye after me, and I will make you fishers of men. And they straightaway left the nets and followed him.'

Matthew 4. 18-20.

Christ stands on dry land and calls to Peter and Andrew who are at sea fishing. The boat is masted with stays, and the sail is furled on the yard-arm. Peter and Andrew each have a hand on the net which they are raising from the water. Andrew has his right hand raised as though greeting Jesus or accepting the call. Part of a saltire cross is seen carved behind his head. Peter in his left hand holds a very large key resting on the gunwales where the rowlocks would be. In medieval iconography the key for St Peter and the saltire cross for St Andrew are these saints' essential attributes. Christ is barefoot. He has long golden hair and a small golden beard. He wears a long pleated gown with capacious sleeves and in his right hand he holds an orb.

tomb and Caiaphas and Annas the other. One of the priests carries a bag of wax and the other seems to be applying his signet ring to the wax placed on the tomb.

In the Brome play of *Abraham and Isaac* (Brome is a small Suffolk village south of Diss), Abraham covers Isaac's face with a cloth to lessen the boy's fear of the descending sword. There are two bosses on this theme (NC8, NC10 p.52). In neither are Isaac's eyes covered, but in the smaller boss (NC8) Abraham has placed his left hand over Isaac's face, and has very deliberately turned aside his own head as he raises his sword. In the *N-Town* version, at this point in the drama, Isaac says to his father:

'and turn from me your face away
my head when that ye shall off smite.'

Next to the Sealing of the Tomb is a boss showing the three Marys coming to the empty tomb (CNA2). The tomb is rectangular: the base ornately decorated with quatrefoils painted in red and gold. The lid lies slant-wise across the top and on its surface is carved a foliate cross on a stepped base. Such a tomb might well have been seen inside the cathedral at this time, Sir Thomas Erpingham's (d.1428) for example. An angel stands to the left of the tomb. The four soldiers are at the foot of the tomb. They are all bearded, helmeted, gorgeted and well armed. All have their eyes wide-open, as though they are aware of what is going on but are powerless to do anything about it. The contorted position of their bodies tells of their agitation and emphasizes the mystery and dynamism of the moment of Christ's resurrection. One of the soldiers grasps an axe with his right hand and puts his left hand to his ear as though scarcely crediting what he hears. Another has his right hand held to his ear. In the *Resurrection* from the *N-Town Play* the four soldiers guarding the tomb have to report to Pilate. The Third Soldier gives his account of the resurrection as follows:

Yea, it was not time then to boast

For when his body took again the ghost

He would have scared many a host,

King, knight and knave,

Yea, when he from the tomb did break

Then was there such an earthquake

That all the world began to shake

And made us all to rave.

Among the most dramatic bosses in the cathedral are those concerning Herod the Great and Herod Antipas. In the plays they are both portrayed as raging tyrants. Herod the Great, the slayer of the small children, in the *N-Town Play*, at the moment when he thinks he has rid himself of the infant whom prophecies say will be even greater than he, is struck by Death's spear, and with his 'knights' is carried off to hell by Satan and his devils. The liveliest north transept bosses portray Herod in a rage with a red demon peeping out above his crown (NTW15, NTE15, NTE21). His counsellors read him the prophecies while he sits in fury and fear, cross-legged tugging at his black forked beard, or having his pulse taken by his physician (NTE23). When the Magi leave his presence his back is turned to them as though he is immediately plotting his next dark scheme. There are two scenes at his deathbed. In the first he lies naked in bed apart from his crown, from which a red devil leers (NTW22 p.121). On one side of the bed sit three of his toadying courtiers who drop crocodile tears at his departure. At the moment of his death (NTC24) three devils in hideous bestial forms reach over the bed to pluck his soul, in the form of a naked child with deformed feet, from out of his mouth so that they can carry it off to hell.

Herod Antipas marries his brother Philip's wife, Herodias. John the Baptist denounces the marriage as contrary to Jewish law. Salome, Herodias's daughter, dances before Herod. As a reward she asks for the head of John the Baptist served on a charger, a large dish. The story caught the

overleaf
Christ healing Peter's mother-in-law
(STW22)

'Now Simon's wife's mother lay sick of a fever; and straightway they tell him of her: and he came and took her by the hand, and raised her up; and the fever left her, and she ministered unto them.'

Mark 1. 30, 31.

This boss is to be found in the south transept where the carvings tell the story of the early part of Christ's ministry. In this transept Christ is usually depicted as boyish, with long hair sweeping over his shoulders, and carrying an orb in one of his hands. Here he is seen with the orb in his left hand, and with his right hand he grasps the wrist of Peter's mother-in-law (Simon who is called Peter). She is sitting, propped up by pillows, in bed. The veil over her head covers her shoulders as well. Her right hand is at her breast. A once white sheet is turned down over her waist. The coverlet is red with golden diapers. On the left stands Peter who holds up his cloak with his right hand and in his left hand holds across his body an enormous key.

The interior scene is set beneath an arched roof with a tie-beam. A five-panelled doorway is at Christ's back. The exterior walls of the house show the details of the stonework. The boss is not deeply carved, giving more the impression of a cartoon.

imagination. Plays on the subject were popular but no extant English version survives. Guilds of St John the Baptist were formed throughout the country, including Norwich in which there were two churches dedicated to him. Salome's dance, in paintings and carvings, is portrayed in a sexually provocative way. In the south transept boss (STC19) she is doing a ritual sword dance as though at the end of the dance the sword will be used to sever John the Baptist's head. The severing of the head is graphically shown in an almost undamaged cloister boss (CSG4). In the south transept series, the head itself on a charger is passed from executioner to Salome and from Salome to Herodias.

The mystery plays end with a representation of the Last Judgement in which Christ from his throne through his trumpeting angels calls all good and evil souls together, and the good who have responded in their lives to the six corporal acts of mercy (Matthew 25) are welcomed into heaven, but the evil, who have neglected these good works, are condemned to hell. The roof bosses in the vaulting of the last bay in the nave give as vivid a picture as the drama. Both forms bring home the fearful consequences of sin, but both retain an element of humour. Pot-bellied devils with bat ears strut in front of their catch of evil souls as they are led in to hell with the scratch marks of the devil's claws about their bodies (NN6). The barmaid who always serves false measures is taken into hell on the devil's back, naked and cheerful, waving her tankard high above her head. The devil is pushing a wheelbarrow in front of him in which sits a naked damned soul, so fearful of his fate that he keeps his hands over his eyes (NN7 p.113). The barmaid or as she is more frequently called 'the unjust alewife', is always a sure candidate for hell and appears as such in one of the versions of the *Chester Mystery Plays*.

The relationship between the fifteenth-century plays in Norwich performed under the auspices of St Luke's Guild and the *N-Town Play* remains a matter for speculation. The scribe of the *N-Town Play* has been located as living a few miles south of Norwich. The cycle is noted for its scholarly and theological content and for the inclusion of a substantial number of plays dealing with the early life of the Virgin Mary. When in the fourteenth and fifteenth centuries the vaulting in the cloisters and nave of Norwich Cathedral was being constructed the cult of the Virgin Mary was growing in popularity. The Lady Chapel at Ely with its iconography of the life of the Virgin and the miracles associated with her, splendidly carved, abundantly illustrated, but now so sadly mutilated, testifies to that popularity. Norwich had its great Lady Chapel and St Anne's Chapel, now lost, and also the Chapel of Our Lady of Pity which still carries in its roof bosses a tribute to the Virgin Mary, carved at about the time when performances of the mystery plays were at their height. The *Purification of the Virgin* within the *N-Town Play* is dated 1468. In the south, west, and north walks of the cloisters are sequences of carvings in which the Virgin Mary is honoured. Norwich itself was on the pilgrims' route to the shrine of Our Lady of Walsingham, after St Thomas of Canterbury's the most visited shrine in the country. A succession of kings and queens made pilgrimages to the Walsingham shrine, some coming several times. Summer was the time of pilgrimage and summer was the time of the open-air public performances of the mystery and morality plays. Although the majority of the iconography associated with the Virgin Mary in Norwich Cathedral has been lost there is sufficient remaining on that theme and others on which to make analogies between the carving of the Norwich roof bosses with the drama produced in the region at the same time.

Although saddened by the mutilation, we should take comfort from the carvings that remain in the cloisters. They illustrate so clearly the craftsman's skill in depicting the age in which he lived, and the faith by which he lived. In many cases there are the closest parallels to be drawn between the carving and what now remains of the drama of the Middle Ages. In the nave and transepts, however, where vandalism and the damage by weathering have been minimal, we still possess a clear and glorious record that is not only closely analogous to the drama of the time, especially the mystery plays, but a work of art which was quite possibly carved and painted by the craftsmen who participated in that drama, and perhaps, more nearly and fully than any other form of visual art, gives clues to an understanding of the drama, its colour and life, its stylistic conventions, its attention to detail, and the buoyancy of its spirit, which only the most stringent measures of Church and State, taken in the latter part of the sixteenth century, were successful in suppressing.

The suppression of religious drama in England took effect at the same time as the first professional theatre opened its doors in London (1576). The stories told in the roof bosses of Norwich Cathedral, stories of birth and death, of grace and damnation, were to be freshly interpreted in the secular drama of Renaissance England.

opposite View from the south-west corner of the cloisters

Acknowledgements

We should like to thank the following for their help in our work which has been many years in preparation: George and Jenny Allison, John Bateman, Colin Bennett, Camilla Boodle, Paul Burbridge, the late Keith Darby, Robin Eaton, Tony and Jane Eggleston, Rachel Farrar, Trevor Forrest, Ray Hall, Ken Harvey, Auberon Hedgecoe, Sebastian Hedgecoe, Stephen Heywood, Walter Lassally, Leica Cameras Limited, the late Andrew Martindale, Michael McLean, Mary Norwak, Colin Pordham, Norman Scarfe, Tim Spurrell, John Stevens, Sheila Upjohn.

Our thanks are also accorded to a number of charitable trusts for helping to fund particular aspects of our work: The Dean and Chapter of Norwich Cathedral, the British Academy, the Esmee Fairbairn Charitable Trust, the Greene Settlement, the Idlewild Trust, the Morgan Blake Charitable Trust, the Pennycress Trust, the Pilgrim Trust, the Norwich Town Close Estate Charity.

Lastly, we are grateful for the enthusiasm and vigour of the Very Reverend Stephen Platten, Dean of Norwich, in so actively supporting this publication.

MARTIAL ROSE
JULIA HEDGECOE

Selected Bibliography

ALEXANDER, J. and BINSKI, P. (ed)   *Age of Chivalry: Art in Plantagenet England 1200-1400*, London 1987.

ANDERSON, M. D.   *The Medieval Carver*, Cambridge 1935; *Drama and Imagery in English Medieval Churches*, Cambridge 1963; *History and Imagery in British Churches*, Edinburgh 1971.

ATHERTON, I. et al. (ed)   *Norwich Cathedral: Church, City and Diocese 1096-1996*, London 1996.

BEADLE, R.   *The Medieval Drama of East Anglia: Studies in Dialect, Documentary Records and Stagecraft* (2 vols). Unpublished D.Phil Thesis, Univ. of York 1977.

BORG, A. et al.   *Medieval Sculpture from Norwich Cathedral*, Norwich 1980.

CAVE, C. J. P.   *Roof Bosses in the Transepts of Norwich Cathedral*, Oxford 1933; *Roof Bosses in Medieval Churches*, Cambridge 1948.

DAVIS, N.   *Paston Letters and Papers of the Fifteenth Century*, Oxford 1976.

SELECTED BIBLIOGRAPHY

DUTKA, J.   *Mystery Plays at Norwich: Their Foundation and Development*, Leeds Studies in English, 1978; *The Lost Dramatic Cycle of Norwich and the Grocers' Play of the Fall of Man*, Review of English Studies No. 137, 1984.

ECCLES, M. (ed)   *Ludus Coventriae: Lincoln or Norfolk?*, Medium Aevum 1971.

FERNIE, E. C. and WHITTINGHAM, A. B.   *The Early Communar and Pitancer Rolls of Norwich Cathedral Priory with an account of the Building of the Cloister*, Norwich 1972.

FERNIE, E. C.   *Norwich Cathedral*, Oxford 1993.

GOULBURN, E. M. and SYMONDS, H.   *On the Ancient Sculptures in the roof of Norwich Cathedral*, London 1876.

GRACE, M.   *Records of the Gild of St. George in Norwich 1389-1547*, Norwich 1937.

HARVEY, J.   *English Medieval Architects*, London 1954; *Cathedrals of England and Wales*, London 1974.

HENRY, A. (ed)   *The Mirour of Mans Salvation: A Middle English Translation of Speculum Humanae Salvationis*, Aldershot 1986.

Biblia Pauperum: A Facsimile Edition, Aldershot 1987.

JAMES, M. R.   *The Sculptures in the Lady Chapel at Ely*, London 1895; *The Sculptured Bosses in the Roof of the Bauchun Chapel of Our Lady of Pity*, Norwich 1908; *The Apocryphal New Testament*, Oxford 1926; *The Apocalypse in Art*, London 1931; *The Sculptured Bosses in the Cloisters of Norwich Cathedral*, Norwich 1911.

LASKO, P. and MORGAN, N. J. (ed)   *Medieval Art in East Anglia 1300-1520*, Norwich 1973.

PEVSNER, N.   *The Leaves of Southwell*, London 1945.

RICKERT, M.   *Painting in Britain in the Middle Ages*, London 1965.

SANDLER, L. F.   'The Hybrid in Manuscript Marginalia', An essay in *Art the Ape of Nature*, New York 1981.

SPECTOR, S. (ed)   *The N-Town Play*, Oxford 1991.

STONE, L.   *Sculpture in Britain in the Middle Ages*, London 1955.

TRISTRAM, E. W.   *The Cloister Bosses: Norwich Cathedral*, Norwich 1935, 1936, 1937.

WAYMENT, H.   *The Windows of King's College Chapel*, Corpus Vitrearum Medii Aevi, Great Britain London 1972

WHITTINGHAM, A.   *Norwich Cathedral Bosses and Misericords*, Norwich 1981.

WILSON, J. (ed)   *900 Years: Norwich Cathedral and Diocese*, Norwich 1996.

WOODMAN, F. S. (ed)   *King's College Chapel*, London 1986.

List of Illustrations

The Fall (NA11) (front cover)
View of a section of the nave vaulting (Bay NA) (back cover)
Green Man (CEM5) 9
The Carrying of the Cross (CED5) 12
A thief stealing the washing (CED4) 13
Man fighting a dragon (CEF3) 16
Tumbler (CEF6) 17
St John and the angel (CSC2) 20
Opening the fourth seal (CSF1) 21
The angel sounds the sixth trumpet (CS15) 24
The sealing of the tomb (CNA5) 25
The Serpent tempting Adam and Eve (CWA1) 28
The Christian of Constantinople (CWJ7) 29
Doubting Thomas (CNB2) 32
The martyrdom of St Denis (CNJ7) 33
The swan (NA15) 36
The eagle (NA16) 37
God blessing his Creation (NA4) 40
Noah building the ark (NB4) 41
Noah's ark (NB11) 44
Carrying the animals into the ark (NB8) 45
Woman carrying birds into the ark (NB13) 48
Noah's vineyard (NB18) 49
Abraham about to sacrifice his son, Isaac (NC10) 52
Abraham's angel (NC11) 53
Isaac, Esau, and Jacob (NC15) 56
Jacob journeys to Paddan-aram (ND4) 57
Jacob wrestles with an angel (ND7) 60
Jacob peeling his roads (ND10) 61
The flight of Jacob's wives (ND17) 64
The marriage of Jacob and Rachel (ND11) 65
Joseph put into a pit by his brothers (NE10) 68
Corn in Egypt (NF1) 69

Moses in the bulrushes (NF4) 72
The Israelites rejoice at their deliverance from Pharaoh (NF9) 73
Samson and Delilah (NG3) 76
David and Goliath (NG4) 77
King Solomon (NG18) 80
David and Solomon (NG15) 81
Pharoah drowning in the Red Sea (NF10) 84
Two shepherds of the Nativity (NH14) 85
The Presentation (NH7) 88
The Nativity (NH10) 89
Christ and the doctors (NI4) 92
Cana (NI7) 93
The feast at Bethany (NI18) 96
The Last Supper (NJ10) 97
Two disciples prepare to have their feet washed (NJ15) 100
Christ before Pilate (NK10) 101
Malchus' ear (NK17) 104
The Buffeting of Christ (NK15) 105
Dicing for Christ's garment (NL7) 108
Mixing vinegar and gall (NL8) 109
The Crucifixion (NL10) 112
The unjust alewife (NN7) 113
Good souls being led into heaven (NN16) 116
The Last Judgement (NN10) 117
The three shepherds come to Bethlehem (NTC18) 120
The death of Herod (NTW22) 121
John the Baptist preaching (STC12) 124
The Holy Innocents (NTC22) 125
The Baptism of Christ (STC5) 128
Christ calling his disciples (STC8) 129
Christ healing the sick (STC22) 132
The calling of Simon and Andrew (STC10) 133
Christ healing Peter's mother-in-law (STW22) 136

Index

Numbers in italics refer to illustration pages

Abel, 67, 70
Abraham, 52, 59, 63, 66, 67, 75, 134
acts of mercy, 58, 137
Adam, *front cover*, 28, 34, 55, 59, 67, 74, 126, 127
alewife, the unjust, 113, 137
Alnwick, Bishop William (1426-36), 87

Angers tapestries, 39
Annas, 25, 42, 134
Anne of Bohemia, wife of Richard II, 118
Annunciation, 35, 55, 114, 118, 119
Antichrist, 39
Apocalypse, 11, 20, 21, 24, 38, 39, 42, 43, 58, 62
Ascension, 59, 78
Assumption of the Virgin Mary, 90, 91, 94

Attegrene, John, 42, 62
Baptism, of Christ, 59, 75, 115, 128
Barnack, 42
Barrabas, 66
Bauchun Chapel, 8, 11, 15, 63, 87, 94, 98, 107
Bauchun, William, 87
Becket, Thomas, Archbishop of Canterbury (1162-70), 11

Bensly, Dr W. T., 110
Bethany, 96
Bethlehem, 118
Biblia Pauperum, 59, 62, 66
Blofield, 62
Bourchier, Thomas, Archbishop of Canterbury (1454-86), 103
Brome Play, 134
Bury St Edmunds, 62
Caen, 7, 8, 27, 42

Caiaphas, 25, 42, 134
Cain, 67, 70, 74, 75
Cain's jawbone, 70, 75
Calvary, 66, 131
Cana, 93
Canterbury Cathedral, 67
Canterbury Tales, 14
Castle of Perseverance, 131
Cave, C. J. P., 110, 111, 119
chapter house, 26, 30, 31
chapel of Our lady of Pity, 54, 78, 90, 94, 138
Chartres Cathedral, 67
Chaucer, 14, 90
Chester Cathedral, 110
Christ, his arrest, 59; before Pilate, 78, *101*; buffeting of, *105*; burial of, 131; calling his disciples, 115, *129*, *133*; carrying the cross, *12*; circumcision of, 115; early life of 115; healing the sick, *132*, *136*; his enthronement, 59, 82; ministry of, 78, 115; resurrection of, 31, 35, 66, 78, 134; temptation of, 115; with the doctors, 92
Clipsham, 27
Coltishall, 54
communar rolls, 42, 87
Corfe, Dorset, 42
Coronation of the Virgin, 90, 91, 94
Courtauld Institute of Art, 43
Cross, the carrying of, 31
Crucifixion, 31, 59, 75, *112*
Danes, 35
David, 59, 75, 77, *81*, 91
David and Goliath, 77, 126, 127
Delilah, *34*
doctors in the temple, 92, 122
Dicing, *108*
Domitian, 39
empress (Bauchun Chapel), 90, 91, 94, 95
Eborard, Bishop (1121-45), 7
Eden, 71, 126
Edward I, King (1272-1307), 26
Edward IV, King (1461-83), 51, 70, 71
Egypt, 63, 118
Eleanor, wife of Edward I, 26
Elizabeth, mother of John the Baptist, 38
Ely Cathedral, 18, 62
Ely, Reginald, 54, 55
Emmaus, 42
Esau, 56
Everard, Robert, 54
Erpingham Gate, 26, 63
Erpingham, Sir Thomas, 134
Eton College, 18
Eton College Chapel, 14, 63, 90
Eve, *34*, 55, 59, 74, 126
executioners, 78

Exeter Cathedral, 10, 110
Exeter College, Oxford, 51
Flagellation, 31
Flight into Egypt, 111, 115, 118
Fox, Bishop Richard, of Winchester (1501-29), 55
Fygot, Francis, 127
Gabriel, 118
Gesta Romanorum, 90
Goldwell, Bishop James (1472-99), 14, 51, 87, 98, 99, 103, 106, 107
Goliath, 127
Goulburn, Dean E. M., of Norwich (1866-89), 15, 111
Green Man, 9
Green Men, 10, 35, 63
grocers, of Norwich, accounts, 126, 127; Guild, 126, 127
Hall, Richard, 42
Hamlet, 70
Handel, 75
Harrowing of Hell, 31, 34
Harvey, John, 32, 98
hell-mouth, 79
Henry II, King (1154-89), 43
Henry IV, King (1399-1413), 71
Henry VI, King (1422-61), 51, 54, 63, 71
Herod the Great, 114, 119, *121*, 130, 131, 135
Herod Antipas, 115, 135
Herodias, 119, 137
Holkham Bible Picture Book, 74
Holy Family, 119
Horne, John, 42
Hue, Simon, 42
iconoclasm, 34
Isaac, 56, 59, 66, 75, 134
Jacob, 56, 57, 59, 60, 61, 65, 67, 75
James, M. R., 90, 111, 114, 115
Joseph, 59, 67, 68, 69, 75
King's College Chapel, Cambridge, 18, 54, 55, 59, 63, 66
Lady Chapel, Ely Cathedral, 54, 138
Lady Chapel, Norwich Cathedral, 54, 78, 138
Lakenham, Prior Henry (1289-1310), 27
Lamech, 70
Last Judgement, 59, *117*, 137
Last Supper, 59, 75, 97
Lazarus, 78
Leman, 127
Leviathan, 34
lierne vaulting, 54, 58, 87
Lincoln Minster, 62
Lollards, 87
Losinga, Bishop Herbert de (1094-1119), 7
Luttrell Psalter, 30

Lyhart, Bishop Walter (1446-72), 11, 51, 54, 71, 83, 98, 107, 111, 115
Magi, 78, 114, 115, 131
Malchus, *104*
Mankind, 131
Man of Law's Tale, 90
Margaret de Bohun, 71
Mary, the Virgin, 35, 43, 55, 58, 63, 78, 79, 111, 118, 138
Marys, the three, 134
Massacre of the Innocents, 114, 118, 131
Methushael, 67
Moriah, land of, 66
Moses, 55, 67, 72, 75
Nathan, 75
Nativity, 59, 78, 89, 114, 131
Nero, 39
Noah, *41*, 49, 59, 67, 75
Noah's ark, *41*, *44*, 59
Noah's Ship, 126
Norfolk and Norwich Archaeological Society, 110
Nykke, Bishop Richard (1501-36), 8, 14, 107, 110, 111, 115
N-Town Play, 70, 131, 134, 135, 138
Ormesby Psalter, 30
Oriel College, Oxford, 51
Paradise, 126, 127
Passion of Christ, 31, 34, 42
Paston, Sir John (1473), 130
Paston, Sir John II (1478), 130
Paston Letters, 130
Patmos, 39
Pentecost, 79
Percy, Bishop Thomas (1355-69), 95
Pharaoh, 66, *84*,. 118
Pilate, 25, 42, 66, *101*, 131
Pole, William de la, 51
Pope's Chancery, 103
post-resurrection themes, 42
Presentation in the Temple, 88, 115
Prior's Door, 31, 34
Purification, 138
Rachel, 64, 65
Ramsey, John, 42
Ramsey, William, 42
Reformation, 18, 27, 39, 110
Red Sea, 66, 91
Reppys, William, 42
Rheims Cathedral, 39
Richard II, King (1377-99), 71, 118
riots of 1272, 8, 26, 54
Roof Bosses in Medieval Churches, by C. J. P. Cave, 110
Roof Bosses in the Transepts of Norwich Cathedral by C. J. P. Cave, 110
St Anne's Chapel, 78, 138
St Anthony's Hospital, 51

St Clement, 43
St Denis, *33*, 43
St Edmund, 35
St Edward, 43
St George's (Tombland, Norwich), 26
St John the Baptist, 31, 114, 115, 119, 122, *124*, 135, 137
St John the Baptist's Guild, 137
St John the Divine, 39, 114
St Joseph, 111, 118, 119
St Laurence, 43
St Luke, 123
St Luke's Guild, 123, 127
St Michael, 39
St Peter, 31
St Paul's, London, 18
St Stephen's, Westminster, 18
St Thomas of Canterbury, 43
St Thomas, 32
Salmon, Bishop John (1299-1325), 27
Salome, 119, 135
Samson, 75, 76
Satan, 34, 74, 127
scourgers, 78
sealing the tomb, 134
Sekyngton, William, 87, 94
serpent, 127
shepherds, 78, *85*, 114, 115, *120*
shrine of Our Lady of Walsingham, 138
shrine of St Thomas of Canterbury, 138
Smiths' Guild, 126, 127
Soldiers, 78
Solomon, 75, *80*, *81*
Southwell Minster Chapter House, 30
Speculum Humanae Salvationist, 59, 62, 66
Stamford, 42
Suffolk, Duke of, 51
Tasburgh, 62
Tewkesbury Abbey, 11
Thetford, 7
Tombland, Norwich, 26
Trinity, the Holy, 70, 82
Tristram, Prof, E. W., 43
Tybnam, Jeffrey, 127
Virgin in Glory, 102
Wakering, Bishop John (1415-1425), 27
Westminster Abbey, 38, 62
Whetley, John, 130
Winchester Cathedral, 10, 62, 110
Wisdom, 131
Woderove, James, 42, 62
Woderove, John 42, 62
Yarmouth, 26
York Minster, 38, 62, 67